D1220244

UNLUCKY:

*A Season of Struggle
in Minor League
Professional
Soccer*

DAVE UNGRADY

SPORTS PUBLISHING INTERNATIONAL
New Market, Maryland

Sports Publishing International

UNLUCKY:
A Season of Struggle in Minor League Professional Soccer

Sports Publishing International / January 1999

All rights reserved.

Copyright © 1999 by Dave Ungrady

Cover and book design by Jeff Thoreson, Sports Publishing International

ISBN 0-966850-0-1

Sports Publishing International
Printed in the United States of America

CONTENTS

"A tremendous educational soccer experience. My game was thoroughly tested and assessed."

-Dave Ungrady

The author of *"Unlucky: A Season of Struggle in Minor League Professional Soccer"* attended Soccer Academy's Adult Residential Camp in 1995. "If I can do it, you can do it"

The Soccer Academy's
Adult Residential Soccer Camp

in its sixth year
For men and women at least 20 years of age
July 11 to July 16, 1999
at Western Maryland College in Westminster, Maryland
Three levels
• Advanced   • Intermediate   • Beginners

After evaluation by camp instructors,
campers choose their level of participation
Fee to be determined
Camp cost includes
• Air-conditioned apartments   • Food   • Massage therapy

For more information, access the Soccer Academy web site at
www.soccer-academy.com, then proceed to adult programs or call

703-385-0150

To the main sources of inspiration in my life:

my mother, who possesses the best creative mind in the family; and

my dad, by far the best athlete in the family.

ACKNOWLEDGMENTS

When you write a book, it helps to have strong and committed support from a team. Let me start with the coach, my business partner Jeff Thoreson. Jeff kept the project in line with practical business advice and a friendly ear. He also coordinated the book's printing and design and produced its layout.

Writer and photographer Bill Kamenjar took all the action photographs for the book and most of the others. Bill also thought of the book's title. Brian Straus, an aspiring writer with an unparalleled passion for soccer, provided very able research, conducted several interviews—including with USISL Commissioner Francisco Marcos—and provided game reports when I was unable. Joyce Frank assisted in the book's front cover design. Copy editor Kathy Drennan worked many long hours and even interrupted some holiday time to make sure the copy was clean and full of clarity. And thanks to dynamic designer Nancy Lambrides, a good friend who offered great guidance in the book's design.

It's important to note that those who helped produce the book did so without any payment up front. The team as a whole accepted a certain risk, and for that, I am tremendously grateful.

Thanks to Gil Castilla, former owner of the Washington Mustangs, for his time and support.

A few author friends and soccer media representatives came off the bench to offer much needed advice and guidance. They include Pulitzer Prize-winning writer Jeffrey Marx and former *Washington Post* colleague Christine Brennan as well as noted soccer publishers and writers Tim Nash and Michael Lewis. USISL media representatives Brian Chenault and Chad Harmon provided tremendous informational support despite my often unrealistic requests. Thanks to Jim Moorhouse, Brian Remedi, Keir

Cochran and their assistants in the Communications Office of the U.S. Soccer Federation. Rick Lawes and Mike Kammerman of D.C. United's Communication Department also deserve a pat on the back for their help.

One other team deserves much thanks for putting up for several months with my presence at games and practices as well as in locker rooms and meetings. I applaud Royals owner Mo Sheta for having such an open mind for allowing me to follow his team so closely. Not enough can be said for the congeniality, enthusiasm and accommodating spirit of Royals head coach Silvino Gonzalo. I thank assistant coach Matt Badiee for his support on the field and for helping me believe that one is never too old to play soccer with an undying passion. Thanks also to part-time assistant Patrick Berkebile and director of operations John Ormassa for assisting with my travel and other logistical needs.

A few people who helped keep me on the field when injuries and other physical discomforts flared up also deserve recognition: Dr. Scott Muzinski at the Arlington Chiropractic Health Center in Arlington, Virginia; Dr. William Booker and Dr. John R. Doepper along with their staff therapists, Melissa Navarro and Jorge Obando, at Capitol Rehab in Arlington; and Sharon Moore and Jodi Scholes at the Northern Virginia Massage Center in Vienna.

I'd also like to thank a few soccer coaches who have managed to teach me a few things about life and athletics. John Wagner, who coached the varsity soccer team my junior and senior years at Notre Dame High School in Trenton, New Jersey to state titles, was by far the best motivational coach in my life. My high school track coaches Gary Dambro and Dave Milinowicz taught me the values of a hard work ethic that I hope to never forget. I am indebted to my college track coaches, Stan Pitts and Frank Costello, for teaching me much about life and for giving me the chance to forge my most memorable athletic moments.

Finally, the Royals players. You may not have realized it as the season progressed, but your individual professional lives and athletic pursuits combined to make one hell of a compelling story. And although you struggled, the challenges you endured can only make you stronger. Thanks for letting me grow along with you.

INTRODUCTION

I drove away from the Northern Virginia Royals media day with heightened anticipation. The event was not successful—I was one of only two media representatives who showed up. But it had given me an idea. The idea was to write a book documenting the team's first season. If the media day event was any indication, the inaugural season for the Royals should prove very interesting.

Then another thought pumped adrenaline through me with the pace of a flooded river. Why stop at just writing? Why not train with the Royals? Why not see if I could get in a game? After a lifetime of dreaming, this was my chance to finally, if fleetingly, become a professional athlete!

After I got home I immediately called Royals owner Mo Sheta. I knew Sheta from playing in the Northern Virginia Soccer League, a top amateur league in the Washington, D.C. area. Sheta sponsored two teams in that league. Sheta said it was okay with him, but I would need to get approval from head coach Silvino Gonzalo.

Two days later, I approached Gonzalo with the idea of the book. It was before the Royals played a scrimmage against Georgetown University. I was immediately struck by his warm personality. As his players made final preparations to start the game, he talked to me near the bench as if he had known me for years.

"Yes, I think that is a good idea," he said. "We would love to have you."

I didn't expect it to be so easy. The next question was the more difficult part. I asked him if I could train with the team so I could get a true feel of what it was like to play for a first-year minor league professional team. I said I needed access to meetings and locker rooms. I wanted to travel with the team on road trips. I told him I didn't expect to be good enough to play in a game and help the team, but I would practice with the intent of getting in a match.

"You never know what happens," he said, with a smile. "Don't sell yourself short. You could be better than everybody out here." His intent was clear. They would look at everybody who wanted to try.

I spent the following five months obsessed with the adventures of a fledgling professional soccer team and my attempt to finally become a professional athlete, something I have desired since I could first read *Sports Illustrated* magazine about 35 years ago. I was a frustrated jock whose soccer and track and field careers in college were hampered by injury. I felt I never reached my potential in either sport. That frustration fueled my ambitions to keep playing highly competitive sports, even as I turned 40 and my aging body continuously defied the rationality of such ambition.

I credit my development as a participatory and behind-the-scenes writer to two authors. The first significant book I remember reading, as a prepubescent sports junky in the mid 1960s, was George Plimpton's *Paper Lion*, an entertaining account of his attempt to play as a quarterback with the pro football Detroit Lions.

As I got older and became a writer, I became intrigued by John Feinstein's behind-the-scenes and compelling books about high profile sports teams, leagues and athletes. My first job out of college in the early 1980s was as a news aide in the *Washington Post* sports department. Feinstein at that time was a budding reporter known for his in-depth features and profiles and a work ethic unmatched in the business. I admired his professionalism and style — he occasionally walked around the newsroom in sock-clad feet and ruffled hair and dressed like a disheveled coach.

As I wrote this book, I used as my inspiration the elegant and jovial prose of George Plimpton and the gritty news gathering and reporting skills of John Feinstein. I hope the result just barely reflects the fine works of these two writing icons.

A final motivating factor for this book was the athlete. I have little sympathy for professional athletes who complain about poor coaching or management decisions and who have trouble making ends meet on millions of dollars a year in salaries.

Professional soccer players are a different story. The average weekly salary for a player in the National Basketball Association is about $40,000.

The average annual salary for a player in Major League Soccer is about $70,000. The most a player is paid in D3, the lowest level of professional soccer in the U.S., is about $10,000 for a season.

Some may read this book and say this is not a fair account of professional soccer in the U.S. Most professional soccer players in the U.S. are paid, although the Royals players were not. But I sensed there would be a more compelling story with a first-year team. I wanted to discover how they mixed work and play, how they managed their love for the game in such challenging conditions and what they were willing to endure to achieve their ambitions.

Another reason I wanted to document the efforts of a first-year D3 team was because I felt that my chances of playing for a more established team, with more player stability, were slim to none.

Typical of an elite athlete, I was being selfish. If you want to be like one, you need to think like one.

Those knowledgeable with the soccer vernacular will understand the title of this book. "Unlucky" in soccer refers to a good effort gone awry. Good hustle, but not good enough. In other words, nice try.

That's what the first season for the Northern Virginia Royals was all about.

1
BY THE LIGHT OF THE MOON

A full moon hung conspicuously in the clear night sky, casting its lunar spell on the soccer setting below. The season and home opener for the Northern Virginia Royals was about to commence, and, by night's end, it would appear affected by a full-moon's supposed effects. A curious subplot had developed even before the game began. John Pascarella, the only member of the Royals at the time who had been on a Major League Soccer roster, fully expected to start the game in goal against the Central Jersey Riptide.

As the opening whistle pierced the chilly, early-spring air, Pascarella sat on the team's bench. He discovered about two minutes before game time that Jan Da Weer would start.

"I've heard two versions," Pascarella said good-naturedly when asked at half time about his field absence. "I was told it might be a player pass problem because I've been in MLS. And I was told by someone else that the coach didn't know I was here. But I was here an hour before the game working with the goalkeeper coach."

He flashed a bemused smile.

"But I'm not going to say anything about it now. I'll sort it out after the game."

He would, sort of.

Da Weer was no rookie to professional soccer, although at lower levels than Pascarella. Da Weer was a prominent keeper for the Washington

Mustangs, the last USISL team to play in the Washington area, and with the now-defunct Baltimore Bays of the USISL. After the Bays folded, some of its players opted to join the Eastern Shore Sharks, also a new USISL franchise, in 1998. Da Weer found no comfort in commuting from the Washington area or moving to play for the Sharks, so he tried out for the Royals and made the squad.

Da Weer strikes a stark contrast to Pascarella. He is shorter, thinner and more reserved than Pascarella. From the sideline, rarely do you hear a word from Da Weer while he's in goal. Pascarella can be so loud it almost sounds like he's standing next to you.

John Pascarella was surprised to learn he was not starting in goal for the home opener.

But Da Weer can clearly make noticeable noise with his keeping skills. He is bolder and quicker off the line than Pascarella. In the home opener he made Royals head coach Silvino Gonzalo look like an early-season candidate for coach of the year. Da Weer played steady throughout the game and made two stellar plays in the first half. During a Central Jersey free kick, he dove high and right and punched the ball away as it sailed toward the top left corner. Later in the first half, he sprinted to just outside the top of the box, won a 50-50 ball against a charging opponent during a breakaway and cleared the ball away with his feet as he slid toward the player. In the second half, Da Weer maintained his aggressive style and ran out close to the near touchline to tackle a player who had gotten behind the defense. He received a yellow card, but prevented what might have been a score.

Da Weer's dramatics stood out in an otherwise uninspiring first half. The Royals, matched up against a team starting its third season in the league, played tentatively and with frayed nerves. Following a scoreless 45 minutes, the team ultimately stirred up some spirited chatter during the half time locker room session.

Gonzalo first addressed a quiet, seemingly dispassionate team.

"A couple things," he said. "First we have to pick it up in the middle. Matt (Ferry, who controls the middle of the field for the Royals), that's your job there. Matt, there's too much space in the middle. We solve that, we beat them. And we need to play more to the left. We'll keep pressing them. They're tired."

Gonzalo's firm words seemed to energize the team.

Sweeper Steven Gill, a burly Brit who was a former apprentice with the Newcastle United Football Club in England, is, at 28, one of the more experienced players on the team. "The butterflies are gone," he said toward the end of half time. "The novelty of our first game is over. Now it's time to go out and play soccer. You know if we come back in here at the end of the game without a win, we'll know we missed a good fuckin' chance. And for those of you who don't play in the back everyday, please be careful in the box."

Gill's admonishment prompted bursts of confident and positive interaction between the players.

One player yelled, "We don't want to go into overtime."

Looking confused, another player then quietly responded, "Is there overtime?"

It was Scott Poirier, a 23-year-old starting forward, who sat calmly throughout most of half time, appearing unconcerned about what was going on. But I would later learn that Poirier's apparent indifference did not mean he was unaware of what it takes to win a close game.

A few minutes into half time I spotted team owner Mo Sheta standing calmly behind the bench and asked how he felt about the sparse crowd of about 400. It was Easter weekend, creating a potential conflict with soccer-enthusiastic followers who believed in Jesus; it was also Passover.

"Not bad for a Good Friday," he said. "A lot of people said they were going away for the weekend."

The crowd was about five times larger than I had expected. I randomly canvassed some soccer acquaintances two weeks prior to the game to gauge their knowledge and interest in the team. The near unanimous response was, "Who? What team?" A preview piece about the team that appeared that morning in *The Washington Post* sports section surely helped increase the crowd size.

The Royals home field is used primarily as a soccer, lacrosse and football field for Fairfax High School. The small crowd barely filled a quarter of the bleachers, but they were passionate and vocal way beyond their numbers.

There was even an annoying — and not very clever — heckler.

"C'mon, Metros rejects. Give it back to us." It was a reference to the opponent's proximity to the New York/New Jersey MetroStars of Major League Soccer. The heckler was a far cry — in creativity and passion — from the loyal following at RFK Stadium, the home field of two-time MLS Champion D.C. United located about 20 miles away.

Something you would never see at a D.C. United game was the random, harmless rowdiness of kids running throughout the bleachers playing tag and rolling down a grassy hill behind one of the goals.

Not that they seemed to care, but the kids were missing a highly entertaining match. Both teams played with more purpose and passion in the second half. The Royals scored first following a foul by New Jersey in the 48th minute. The restart from the left flank floated to the far post. Forward Rick Engelfried headed the cross to the left corner of the goal and the ball bounced in untouched.

Northern Virginia's defense then began to break down. New Jersey's first goal came in the 60th minute after a cross from the right flank rolled across the goal mouth about eight yards out. The Riptide went ahead in the 73rd minute by converting a penalty kick after a handball was justifiably called against the Royals in the box.

The Royals waited to the last minute to force an overtime. With a few ticks more than one minute remaining, Ferry worked 1 v 1 magic on the left flank to steer clear of a defender. Once free, he drilled a low cross through the heart of the box. Engelfried, a former scoring demon at James Madison University, punched in the loose ball just a few yards in front of the goal mouth for his second goal of the match.

Immediately after regulation, most players were confused about what would happen next — an overtime session or a shoot-out. League rules stipulate that a tie game after regulation is followed by a 15-minute sudden death overtime. If the game was still deadlocked after the extra session, the winner would be determined by a shoot-out.

The Royals bench was juiced during the break before the start of overtime. The last-minute goal created a renewed enthusiasm. If their bodies evidenced traces of fatigue, their faces showed a stern focus and unbridled intensity. Their sudden boost of confidence pierced the cold night air with a breeze of controlled arrogance. They felt they had the game in hand. The home opener, which minutes before looked disappointing, was suddenly transformed into a possibly revitalizing conquest.

"That team is tired. That goal they gave up there is the end," shouted Gonzalo as most players stirred excitedly about him.

Assistant coach Matt Badiee used forceful verbiage to encourage midfielder Adam Wilson to stop wandering from his interior midfield position.

"Adam, don't lose your fucking shape again," he said.

Wilson looked inspired rather than threatened.

Right back Chris Jones, one of the more accomplished players on the team, seemed to sense that a basic perspective was needed. He called the players into a huddle before resuming play.

"This is just real simple," he said. "They're all counterattacks. They're too tired, just sticking their legs out."

Most players fought severe fatigue in the overtime session. Not surprisingly, the strategy for both teams appeared to be to get the ball up field as quickly as possible to the fresh-legged, late substitutes who were making long, hard runs and pressuring tired defenders.

Ironically, a player whose work rate had declined considerably early in the second half would muster the final heroic effort for the home side.

When followers of Washington area soccer talk about Scott Poirier's youth career, their words are laced with wonderment. "If only..."; "he could have been..."; "what happened...?"

He was the boy from Fairfax High School with the bomb-like boot, silky skills and an equally explosive and volatile temperament. As a youth, he played for numerous Olympic Development Program (ODP) teams and a U.S. Youth National Team. Many of his young playing peers are members of MLS teams.

ODP is a system set up by U. S. Youth Soccer, the largest youth soccer organization in the U.S., to identify and develop through tryouts the top youth talent in the country. The hope is that someday they will become top adult players and lead the U.S. National Team to international success. Players are picked for state ODP teams, then regional teams and ultimately national teams.

Poirier displayed disciplinary deficiencies in high school and college and, claiming burnout, quit while in college and did not play for nearly four years.

Poirier had been playing again for almost a year before the Royals first game and he showed renewed vigor. He was an active forward in the first half, pressuring the defense, making runs to the corners and withdrawing into the midfield to help defensively. But midway through the second half, he had settled in as a target up front. He failed to convert a couple of good scoring chances from inside the box. He was mostly an afterthought during most of the overtime session. Until the last 70 seconds.

Adam Wilson, one of Poirier's closer friends, had just won the ball on the left flank about 35 yards from goal. He lofted a high cross into the box to no one in particular, hoping that a Royal header or volley would culminate the dream play. The Riptide goalkeeper made a move to knock the ball away, but Poirier beat him to the ball as it floated to the far post. Poirier's forehead directed the ball into the upper right corner as he fell back to the turf, resulting in a stunning winner for the home team. He was immediately smothered by his teammates in a pile of jubilant humanity.

"Scott—you will see him in MLS someday," an exhilarated Gonzalo said a couple minutes after Poirier scored the game winner.

The drama was not over.

The Royals locker room was curiously subdued considering the feat they had just accomplished. Perhaps it was because some of them were saying to themselves, "Yeah, it's a good win, but I've got to go to work tomorrow."

Pascarella, who works full time in the fitness industry, dressed quickly while imparting to me his soccer biography. Long, curly black hair fell wildly just below Pascarella's shoulders. A bushy mustache partially hid a well-chiseled and handsome face. Pascarella owns a degree in exercise physiology and has worked primarily as a fitness director at numerous health clubs for nearly a decade. A sturdy, lean build reflects dedication to his career.

After graduating from Penn State University in 1988, Pascarella played in a professional league in Peru, and for the Washington Stars and the Richmond Kickers of the American Professional Soccer League.

Pascarella signed with the Royals after D.C. United head coach Bruce Arena suggested he find a team that would give him playing time. Pascarella's family is from the Washington, D.C. area and he returned there after leaving the Los Angeles Galaxy in the middle of the 1996 season. Pascarella trained with the Galaxy and was an assistant coach for a couple months. Arena let Pascarella train with United for about two months during the end of the 1997 season.

Pascarella had played only exhibition games for the Galaxy and wanted another chance to prove he was MLS-worthy. He had been training with the Royals since the beginning of preseason and thought he had won the starting position over Da Weer. In fact, he received most of the work in goal during the team's final practice before the game.

Pascarella seems comfortable confronting an uncomfortable situation. I asked him if he had discovered why he didn't start.

"Yeah, I'd like to know," he said, matter-of-factly.

Pascarella then called out to Badiee, who walked over to him.

"Hey, Matty, what happened?" he said. "I've got a wife and family out there. They're gonna ask me what happened. They're gonna say, 'Are you a second-stringer?' If I'm not gonna start, I want to know. I don't have to play. I've got a family, a full-time job. And a house."

He suddenly realized that maybe he was being a bit too confrontational.

"I'm not trying to say I'm threatening to quit."

Badiee listened patiently to Pascarella's concerns and responded calmly. "Well, that's how it sounds to me."

I sensed a building conflict and walked away to allow the coach and player to sort out their differences. Gonzalo soon joined the discussion, to which the other players seemed oblivious. They talked for another 10 minutes, with Pascarella's voice, continuously pleading for clarification, rising slightly above the coaches'.

Soon after the discussion ended, Gonzalo calmly told me why Pascarella had not started. "I thought Da Weer was more prepared for the game," he said. "That's a decision you make as a coach."

A few minutes later I spotted Pascarella talking to friends in the hallway just outside the locker room.

"Got it all worked out?"

"I don't know," he said. "You were there. We'll see what happens."

As I walked to my car, I pondered the dilemmas and subplots that had quickly formed during the first game in Northern Virginia Royals history.

Would John Pascarella be forced to ultimately pursue his MLS dream elsewhere?

Will the volatile Scott Poirier use his late-game heroics as a catalyst to the stellar soccer career many have expected from him?

Do the now somewhat-tested Royals have what it takes to win a title?

How absurd to be thinking title after just one game. Perhaps the full moon had affected my thought patterns.

A COMMITMENT TO THE PLAYERS

T he organizers of the Royals "Meet the Players" press conference in early April 1998 certainly provided the appropriate elements to lure members of the media. Greasy chicken wings, raw vegetables accompanied by a creamy dressing, baked potatoes topped with cheese and bacon chips, and various soft beverages — all free. The restaurant hosting the event, P.J. Skidoos of Fairfax, Virginia, provided the food and the setting, in a spacious, comfortable basement room used for such events. Many journalists would drive in a Yugo from the Eastern Shore during a blizzard for that kind of complimentary fare. But most of the food went uneaten.

I was one of only two media representatives who attended the event. I found out about it from an invitation faxed to my office. The other journalist stayed briefly, chatted with a few people, picked up a media packet and then departed. I do not point this out for personal gain or recognition; rather, that fact served as an undeniable omen. It illustrated and foretold the struggles the Royals would face their first season as they tried to attract respect and media coverage in a saturated sports market with nearly one dozen higher-profiled professional and college sports teams.

After it appeared that the media attendance would not improve, the hostess of the press conference stepped to the podium a couple of times to apologize with more humility than a repentant, prostitute-tempted preacher.

She blamed the small crowd on the Orioles' opening day; she guessed that maybe the media stayed out a bit too late following the Orioles' home opener the night before.

I tried to put a positive spin on the situation. I had unlimited access to a dozen or so players and a handful of management personnel. And when you are the only media representative at a press conference, the pertinent parties approach you. The only problem was that I had no direct affiliation with a daily publication, a periodical that would be interested in a report,

Silvino Gonzalo took the head coaching job not knowing if he would get paid.

or any broadcast outlet that might pick up a sound bite or two. I was there to satisfy my own curiosity about the team. And at that time, I did not think of writing this book.

The first person introduced to me was Silvino Gonzalo, the head coach. I was impressed immediately by his pleasant personality and charm.

Gonzalo, who was born and raised in Spain, had compiled an impressive record as a coach. As a head coach, he led Club Espana of St. Louis, Missouri to a National Men's Amateur Cup title in 1985 and the U.S. Open Cup title in 1987; Iberia of the Northern Virginia Soccer League (NVSL) to the 1996 U.S. National Men's Amateur Cup title; the Virginia Senior Men's Amateur State Team to a Region I Championship and a second place in the 1997 Donnelly Cup. As an assistant coach, he helped the Washington Diplomats win a league title in the American Soccer League in 1988.

It was tougher to gain access to Mo Sheta, the team owner. Players and management had as many questions for him as I did. When we finally had a chance to chat, Sheta was forthright about his approach to the team.

He talked about how he built the team from players he has known for many years and who have played in premier amateur leagues in the D.C. area. Salaries would be as high as $1,000 per month for some players. He said most players have various jobs. Sheta said he handled about five calls a day from players who wanted to try out.

I left the press conference feeling concerned for the team and wondering if Sheta really understood what he was about to embark upon. Minor league professional soccer in the Washington, D.C. area has had less than rousing success.

I observed firsthand the struggles of the first USISL franchise

A pre-practice jog during an early season practice. The Royals brought strong amateur success into their first season.

in Washington, D.C. Washington Mustangs General Manager Gil Castilla, one of three original owners of the team, had seen me host a raffle at a small soccer expo in Rockville, Maryland and asked me to be their public address announcer for their inaugural season in 1994. At the time I was hosting a weekly soccer radio show on WTEM-AM, an all-sports station serving the Washington area.

The Mustangs offered me game tickets and some soccer equipment, but I asked instead for $50 per game. I didn't think Mustangs tickets would carry much worth and, as a struggling free-lance journalist and soccer publisher, cash in hand was more desirable at the time. It also proved hard to collect by the end of the season. The team did not pay me for a couple of games, but I stopped complaining after I discovered that many players did not get paid for the last two months of the season.

Steve Powers was one of those players. He played professional soccer in the U.S. from 1988 to 1994 in four different leagues. A goalkeeper in the mid 1980s for the University of Maryland, Powers helped lead the Maryland Bays to the American Professional Soccer League title in 1990. He was voted the Most Valuable Player of the title game that season.

Powers ended his pro career with the Mustangs, where he played one season and was offered $100 a game.

"After we played about 13 games, I got my first check for seven games," he said. "As the season started winding down and I didn't have the last round of checks, I knew it wasn't going well. I remember getting a check for three games on a Friday night. They asked me to wait until Tuesday to cash it."

He laughed.

"I raced right to the bank and cashed it."

Castilla bought into the Mustangs with fellow owners Jamie Sarmintos, a local contractor, and Alberto Rodriquez, an owner of an automobile repair shop. Castilla, the owner of ABI Construction in Gaithersburg, Maryland, a contractor for commercial real estate, felt it was a low risk investment and was a good opportunity to organize international club games in the Washington, D.C. area.

"It sounded like an opportunity to take soccer to another level," he said. "And I really enjoyed the game."

Castilla's heart was clearly in the game. At Blair High School in Silver Spring, Maryland, he was a *Washington Post* All-Met soccer player and led his team to a state title in 1975. Castilla played three years at the University of North Carolina, Wilmington and earned All-South status there as a junior.

At 35, Castilla was a bit young to be a professional soccer team owner. But he was willing to invest some money in the team. His energy and resourcefulness would prove essential to keeping the team afloat for two of its three years of existence.

Castilla and his fellow investors opted into USISL ownership soon after the league office approached them. They were persuaded in part after watching a Maryland Bays game in 1993 to get a feel for a USISL game. The Bays had switched to the USISL after the American Professional Soccer League folded.

They walked away impressed. "It was a good atmosphere," said Castilla. "The costs seemed reasonable. We started putting our heads together to see how we could structure the thing."

Castilla and his fellow owners worked the numbers: about $23,000 in league costs, including a $13,000 fee to operate a franchise; players' salaries of about $30,000, or $1,500 a game; traveling and per diem costs, some of which were reduced by promotional barters. The investors figured they could get the team started by each contributing about $10,000 or so up front. They hoped that ticket revenue would help pay salaries and miscellaneous expenses.

But the owners soon discovered some hidden costs that Castilla claims they were never told about during the league's sales pitch to lure the ownership group.

His tone became a bit hostile when he recited the hidden costs.

"You paid for some costs to register a player," he said. "They nickeled and dimed you for every yellow and red card. If a referee report said a player had his socks down, they fined you. If you started a game 20 minutes late, they fined you. It was more of an insult than anything else, kind of like when you buy a car. It all sounded good in the beginning."

Operating costs the first year escalated to $110,000, about $40,000 more than expected.

"Every single penny went to the team," said Castilla. "One of the things I'm disappointed about is that the league started out with an agenda and you have no control with what happens. We thought we were buying into a franchise. But—and this is our fault—we discovered that we bought a license to operate in the USISL. It was no different than buying a driver's license."

USISL Commissioner Francisco Marcos confirmed that the Mustangs did in fact buy a license. "They had the exclusive territorial right to operate a business," said Marcos. "They did not share in the profits or losses of other clubs, like Major League Soccer does. They kept all the money they brought in. Legally speaking, they were not called franchise operations. But the practical rights were the same."

Castilla feels Marcos promised more than he could deliver.

"Marcos had us by the balls," he said. "He is a good salesperson. He was selling us castles in the sky. His whole vision was that we were going to be the feeder system to Major League Soccer, that when an MLS team wanted to sign one of our players, we would get a signing bonus. But when MLS started, the teams had their own agenda, different than what everybody had envisioned. D.C. United wanted nothing to do with the Mustangs when they first started."

D.C. United General Manager Kevin Payne said the team considered working with the Mustangs on a limited basis, but he remembers that nothing was done.

"I remember getting a letter from them and I believe we tried to do a few things with them," he said. "But that was our first year. We had a lot on our plate at the time."

Payne says the Mustangs sent a letter requesting to play a game at RFK Stadium before a D.C. United game. But Payne felt that was not feasible. "For us to play an extra full soccer game at RFK costs about $10-15,000," he said. "You have to open the gate two hours before the normal time. You have to pay more for stadium personnel. We couldn't incur that cost."

The Mustangs compiled a respectable first year, finishing 12-8 and making the playoffs, where they lost in the first round.

During its second season, the Mustangs reduced their operating budget to around $50,000 and saved $400 a game by moving their home field to Richard Montgomery High School in Rockville, Maryland. The Mustangs paid $1,200 per game at their previous home site, Washington & Lee High School in Arlington, Virginia.

That year, the Mustangs drew some 4,000 people—its largest home crowd—against the Under-20 Universidad de Catolica, a club team from Chile. A large crowd at that game justified one of Castilla's reasons to buy into the Mustangs. As an owner of a professional team in the Washington, D.C. area, Castilla could work directly with promoters to host international games in the area. Castilla could help the promoter get approval from the U.S. Soccer Federation to stage the match. In turn, Castilla could work out a financial arrangement with the promoter. A promoter can also obtain Federation permission for an international game through a state youth or amateur representative. Castilla said the net earnings for that game were about $5,000.

Still, the Mustangs struggled financially in 1995 and Castilla again lost money. By the end of the second season, he had lost $30,000 in his investment as an owner of the Mustangs.

During the 1995 season, Castilla said league owners were so disenchanted with their inability to own a franchise that they discussed buying out Marcos during an owners meeting in Dallas.

"We wanted to make Marcos an offer and hire him as commissioner," he said. " That way we could control the costs. We wondered where the money was going."

Marcos confirmed that some owners did look into buying a portion of the league and the whole league. "They did negotiate with me," he said. "But at the end of the day they realized that there weren't enough owners remotely interested (in buying him out)."

Mo Sheta took some financial risk when he bought the franchise rights for the Royals.

If the owners were so uncomfortable with how the league was set up, why didn't they bail out?

"You put your heart into a team," said Castilla. "And it hurts after you spend $60-$70,000."

After the 1995 season, Castilla dropped out as an owner of the Mustangs, with his contracting business still intact. The money he invested in the team came from savings.

"It's painful for me to remember this stuff," he said.

When asked if he would own another professional soccer team in the U.S., Castilla responded quickly and pointedly. "If someone came to me and said let's make some money out of soccer, unless I had one million dollars tomorrow and I needed a write-off, I'd say no."

I t was difficult for Mo Sheta to say no to a USISL representative when they contacted him in September 1997 to start a D3 team in the Washington, D.C. area. He first thought about owning a professional team in 1994. He gave the idea serious consideration two years later after his amateur team, Total Sports, lost a U.S. Open Cup game, 5-0, to the Carolina Dynamo, a USISL team. The winner of that game played D.C. United, the eventual champion, in a quarterfinal match.

The demonstrative defeat did not dishearten Sheta. Total Sports was gaining respect as a top amateur team in the U.S. and Sheta was spending thousands of dollars a year to sponsor the team.

"We spent $9,800 the year we won the regional cup with no chance of making money on the team," said Sheta. "We were practicing twice a week. And we were getting tired of playing in the NVSL. It was time to go to the next level."

Sheta started playing the game at age 3 in soccer schools in his native country of Egypt. He came to the U.S. at 13 and continued playing soccer, ultimately for varsity teams at Oakton High School, George Mason University and the University of the District of Columbia. In the early 1980s, he played primarily as a sweeper with a reserve team for the Washington Diplomats of the old North American Soccer League and practiced against the likes of Dutch legend Johann Cruyff.

"I was young and didn't take the game too seriously then," he said.

It's hard to imagine Sheta taking anything seriously. A placid personality protects any apparent excessive drive or ambition, which he has used to build a thriving sports recreation business in Woodbridge, Virginia. Sheta owns the Total Sports Pavilion, which hosts leagues for indoor soccer, volleyball, hockey and other sports. He also owns Mo's Sports Shop, a soccer retail store with locations in the Pavilion and in Arlington, Virginia.

Sheta converses softly and comfortably, rarely deviating from his calm tone. During downtime on a Friday afternoon before an early-season night game against the Rhode Island Stingrays, Sheta managed an hour to chat in depth about his plans for his first professional soccer team. We sat at a bar around the corner from the team hotel during a trip to play three games in New England. It was the kind of bar that attracted a strong blue collar element — pseudo sports theme; hard and thick oak bars and wooden stools surrounded by peanut shells; one lone drunk trying to converse annoyingly with whoever would listen.

"I enjoy seeing the guys on the field who I've coached through the years — like Ricky (Engelfried, who sat behind me eating a sandwich and drinking a soft beverage) — getting a chance to play at a higher level," he said.

The Royals were primarily a blending of two top amateur teams from the Washington, D.C. area, Total Sports and Iberia. The two played against each other often in the NVSL Premier Division and in regional amateur tournaments.

"People thought we didn't like each other," said Sheta. "It was tough but it was a clean rivalry. For example, Ricky (Engelfried) played up front for Total Sports against Stevie (Gill), a sweeper for Iberia. I don't think at any time we never shook hands after a game."

After Sheta decided to start a team in the USISL, he contacted Gonzalo to be the coach.

"I wouldn't do it unless he agreed to be the coach," said Sheta. "We knew each other from the NVSL, played against each other for five years. If you asked anybody, we hated each other. But there was never animosity between us. People from the NVSL were surprised that we did this together. But I didn't consider any other coach. He's part of the reason I wanted to do this. He was committed and has given it a lot of time and effort. That's why I didn't go to a lot of practices in the beginning. I have a lot of friends on the team. I wanted them to understand it's his team."

Despite Gonzalo's high level of commitment, Sheta has given him no guarantees.

"There's no contract, no money," he said. "We went into it saying we'll see what happens."

There is also no money for the players. Sheta's initial idea of paying some players changed considerably after the season started.

"I want everybody on the same level," he said. "Either everybody gets paid or nobody gets paid. I don't want somebody to think that they are a superstar. People who come in and don't know me that well, or players who know me but haven't played for me, when they come in and ask 'How much are you paying?' or 'What's the financial situation?' I say we're not going to charge you anything for promoting you as a player or giving you an opportunity, which is usually worth about $5,000 a year."

Sheta answered quickly when he was asked if it was tough to convince players to play for him.

"No," he said. "We have eight players from Total Sports; they've played with me for a long time. They've seen I've tried to do things the right way."

Sheta said if attendance revenue surpassed operating costs, then players would start getting paid. That scenario seemed unlikely for a first-year franchise whose projected operating budget was $150,000.

Sheta ultimately hopes to sell sponsorship packages—mostly from logo exposure on the team uniform—that would reap some $100,000 annually for the team, as well as banner space at games for $150 per game. A sponsor would have to pay $30,000 for exposure on the front of the jersey.

"I told Tim (Schweitzer, a friend who helped with marketing) whatever you can get for this year is fine, but get them on board next year," he said. "That's not a lot of money compared to other teams. The Richmond Kickers (of the A-League, one division up from the D3, in which the Royals participate) get $80,000 for the front of their jerseys." Columbia Hospital provided the Kickers with cash and in-kind services—for example, rehabilitation facilities for injured players—for that sponsorship.

Sheta also hopes to ultimately set up promotional barters for hotel space, gas, food and car rentals.

The only paying sponsor the Royals attracted their first year was Telemundo. The Hispanic television network paid $500 and received a game banner in return.

To be fair, Sheta did not have much time to set up an effective marketing plan for the 1998 season after he decided to start the team in November 1997. Preseason practice was two months away. He needed to find game and practice fields, sign players and set ticket prices and packages.

Sheta initially brought in two other investors, Sherif Shehata—who has known Sheta for a few years—and John Ormassa. Shehata, who owns a vitamin store and a foreign trade company, is the Royals team manager. His primary duties were arranging team trips and negotiating player contracts.

Ormassa's connection to the Royals is more coincidental. Ormassa tried out for the Royals but instead of earning a place on the roster, he won the confidence of Sheta to become the team's director of operations and an assistant coach. In that role, Ormassa would coach the Royals farm team in the Arlington League, an amateur league in the Washington area that features top-quality Hispanic talent.

Ormassa played varsity soccer at Yale in the early 1970s and was elected captain his senior year. He was the leading goal scorer on the team his junior season and on the school's freshman team. Ormassa plays an elegant, if not aggressive, game. The 46-year-old showed often during team practices that he still commands a soft touch with the ball.

But his calling with the Royals would be in the front office. Ormassa had some expendable cash and became a minority owner. Ormassa also invested in Mo's Sports Shop in Arlington.

Ormassa possesses an eccentric personality. He is usually quiet, unassuming to the point of shyness and occasionally seems aloof. Yet, his presence at times provided comic relief. At about mid-season, Gonzalo, Ormassa and I gathered at an Enterprise Car Rental location in Alexandria, Virginia to pick up vans for a trip that day to Roanoke. While I sat in one of the vans waiting for Gonzalo to complete paper work in the office, I noticed an animated Ormassa in between rows of parked cars, shuffling his feet and singing a song as if he was having a flashback to Woodstock. His brief routine certainly cured any boredom that might have started to engulf me.

Early in the season, Ormassa and I shared a ride back to the Washington, D.C. area from a Royals game in Reading, Pennsylvania. After the Friday night game, we started our venture back home about 11 p.m., following an ugly 4-1 loss. Rain was pelting the Reading area as we departed.

Ten minutes into the ride, I noticed that Ormassa had more difficulty navigating the route than usual, due primarily to incessant squinting.

"John, what's with all the squinting?"

"I'm having trouble seeing the signs."

I paused, trying to show some understanding and patience.

"Don't you have glasses, or contacts?"

"Yeah, but I don't like to wear them. They're uncomfortable."

I was a bit dumbfounded. I thought about offering to drive but my night vision isn't much better, even with contact lenses. I opted to just roll with it.

To be fair, I am known as a fairly poor navigator. Due to my lack of concentration, we missed a couple of turns on our way back to the hotel. Poor eyesight (driver) and a poor attention span (navigator) combined for a good chance of getting lost.

After losing our way at least two more times, we completed the normally two-and-a-half hour trip in four-and-a-half hours.

Ormassa was in charge of distributing flyers promoting the team to area youth clubs. Several times during the season, he asked the players after practice to donate some time on weekends to hand out the flyers.

"All of our marketing efforts had poor results," he said after the season. "The weather killed us. The leafleting we did was washed away from the rains. Once we put flyers on about 1,000 cars at a D.C. United game in the spring, but it rained our next home game. And I had little support from the players. Only about five or six helped during two efforts."

Sheta said Royals management contacted youth club presidents and went to club meetings to spread the word about the team.

"If we get 500 a game at $5 a ticket, then we'll be okay," he said. "I think it will happen in a couple of games. I think we can get 1,000 or 1,500 a game."

What would Royals owner Mo Sheta consider successful?

"If we were looking to make money right away, this wouldn't be the thing to do," he said. "The second year I'd like to break even. The third year we need to make money. We did this because when we started we had the commitment of the players. But I'd like to make money."

A FUTURE OF FLUCTUATION

P erhaps it is fitting that the Rochester Raging Rhinos won the 1998 A-League title. With their 3-1 win over the Minnesota Thunder on October 17, 1998, the Rhinos established themselves as the best of Division 2 professional soccer in the U.S. More than 13,000 fans attended the A-League championship game, played at Frontier Field, the Rhino's home stadium.

The Rhinos have captured the unabashed interest of predominantly white-collar Rochester, a suburban city in northwest New York. And since they first fielded a team in 1996, they've been one of the more successful franchises in U.S. professional soccer history during the last two decades.

In 1996, the Rhinos were the runners-up in the A-League and the U.S. Open Cup, losing to D.C. United in the final. That year, they attracted nearly 15,000 fans to a playoff game. The stadium has since been downsized to accommodate a AAA baseball team.

The Rhinos were part of the A-League until October 1996 when the USISL and the A-League merged to form one outdoor professional group with two divisions-the Division 2 A-League and the D3 Pro League.

In 1997, playing for the first time as a USISL Division 2 A-League team, the Rhinos averaged 9,979 fans at their home games, by far the best in the league. In 1998, they averaged 11,500 per game at Frontier Field.

"It's become a very important family social event in the summertime in Rochester," said Ken Anderson, the media relations coordinator for the Rhinos. "We market to soccer moms and the community. There are a load of youth soccer and amateur players to draw from."

Rochester has become a media Mecca for soccer. Several of the Rhinos' games are broadcast on the Empire Sports Television Network, whose coverage extends to Western Pennsylvania and as far east as Binghamton, New York. All the Rhinos games are broadcast live on radio and worldwide on the Internet. During their season, four soccer shows fill the Rochester radio waves.

Five local television stations—four local network affiliates and one independently-owned, 24-hour cable news station—cover the team regularly; as do two daily newspapers and several community and ethnic newspapers.

"(The success of the Rhinos) gives everybody a pinnacle to shoot for," said USISL Commissioner and founder Francisco Marcos. "It gives us a lot of credibility in the marketplace."

In its first year, the A-League had 24 teams, including the Rhinos. Finally, with the Rhinos, Marcos had obtained a marquee franchise. And finally, Marcos could claim an elite level soccer domain.

Marcos, who speaks five languages, is one of the most renowned soccer entrepreneurs in the U.S. A 1968 graduate of Hartwick College, Marcos began his career in professional soccer as the director of public relations and the vice president of soccer operations for the Tampa Bay Rowdies of the North American Soccer League. He later was the vice president of player personnel for the Dallas Tornado and helped start a North American Soccer League franchise in Calgary, Canada.

In 1986 Marcos founded the Southwest Indoor Soccer League (SISL), which hosted the first indoor amateur and youth tournaments. The SISL was the catalyst for Marcos to eventually develop his current league, the broadly-scoped United Systems of Independent Soccer Leagues (USISL).

While Marcos lauds the resounding success of the Rhinos—they've turned a profit their last two seasons—the Rhinos do not reflect a norm in the USISL, or in professional soccer. "To say Rochester is typical is not true," he said. "It's really a puzzle. The only constant in professional soccer, for sure at (the USISL) level, is fluctuation for the next 10 to 20 years."

Most teams in the USISL do not turn a profit. "Very few teams make money," said Marcos. "Probably only one dozen teams make money, break even or lose very little money."

The USISL boasts close to 150 teams in its five divisions. It includes two national outdoor professional divisions for men, the A-League and D3.

D3 is the largest division in the USISL. It included 39 teams in every region of the U.S. in 1998 and is broken up into seven divisions. The Royals competed in the Atlantic division, the largest division with eight teams.

The USISL also includes a national professional division for women (the W-League), a national amateur division (the Premier Development Soccer League), and a regional professional indoor league (the I-League).

In June 1999, the USISL hopes to debut the Y-League, the first national youth league. The Y-League, for boys' teams U-14 and U-15, will start with four to six "pilot regional areas" that will include from six to eight teams and will be affiliated with the U.S. Youth Soccer Association.

"We would like them to be connected to USISL teams, but it's not mandatory," said Marcos.

With the start of the Y-League, the USISL will comprise the main elements of competitive soccer in the U.S.—adult men and women and youth. Marcos, nicknamed the Portuguese Pitchman for his renowned ability as a salesman, was asked if he had the best support system for soccer in the U.S.

"It is the only one, so by default it is the best," he said. "Is it the ideal one? No."

Ideally, Marcos would like to see two A-League teams located within 100 miles of each Major League Soccer franchise. Several D3 teams would be affiliated with an A-League team within that A-League's region. The USISL is set up as a developmental league for soccer players who want to play in MLS or be a member of the U.S. National Team.

Marcos says it's important that the league develop players, but the top priority is to be profitable. "(Being profitable) is crucial, it's number one, otherwise we have to ask the teams for more money." said Marcos.

To join D3, a team must pay a one-time fee of $35,000 and submit a

$15,000 line of credit. Teams will also pay up to $6,000 in annual league fees.

"When we sell rights (to a team), we are essentially selling a certain amount of exclusivity within a territory," said Marcos. "For example, the Royals have Northern Virginia and Washington, D.C. proper and nobody else can come in there at any level (A-League, D3 or PDSL). But if the Royals want to share a territory, then we'll talk. They have an exclusive territory in which they can conduct their business. They keep all the money that they bring in."

Marcos was the sole owner of the USISL until 1996. Umbro, the soccer equipment company, then purchased 60 percent of the league with Marcos retaining 40 percent. Umbro recently reduced its league ownership to 30 percent. Riddell, the sporting goods and apparel company and Signal, a casual sportswear company, purchased the marketing rights for Umbro in the U.S. Riddell and Signal each own 15 percent of the league.

As Commissioner and President of USISL, Inc., Marcos oversees the day-to-day operation of the league. And his style is very hands-on.

Marcos has implemented a stern system to help maintain league stability. "We ask the teams to literally snitch on everyone else," he said.

Each team receives a rating form to assess other teams' ownership quality, management, the quality of a facility and cooperation from the front office, among others. The results were compiled at the end of the season.

"We will reveal the results to everybody so they can look each other in the eye and say 'Who's the idiot that said that I have no towels in my locker room?'" he said. "We feel that peer pressure and peer review is the most effective tool we've got."

Marcos said half a dozen teams in the A-League were placed on probation following the 1998 season. The Royals were not among them.

"If (teams) don't do what they're supposed to do to have this professionalized image, they will be fined because it is the only thing they understand," he said. "No amount of reprimands will take care of the problem. It is no different than telling your son to stop messing up the table."

While Marcos has built a relatively stable soccer empire, some league critics complain that he is padding his own financial pockets while most teams in the league struggle to make money on their investments.

"In the last three or four years, primarily because of Umbro's involvement, we have been in the black," said Marcos. "But I can argue that during the first six or seven years, nobody bothered to ask me if I made a profit."

One USISL team that's been able to turn a profit from the beginning is the Kalamazoo (Michigan) Kingdom of the PDSL. Chris Keenan and his wife, Stephanie, purchased the team in 1996 for $22,500. They say it is now worth $300,000. In their three years of existence, they've become a model USISL team.

The Keenans have used a savvy business approach in an ideal PDSL market to develop one of the USISL's more successful franchises. The roster includes either college players looking to keep their games sharp during the off-season or local high school kids trying to develop their games.

"Last season we had three 18-year-olds and the rest were college kids," said Chris Keenan.

During the last two summers, the Kingdom featured about half a dozen players from Indiana University, the 1998 NCAA Tournament champion. Sam Franklin, a starting midfielder at the University of Virginia in 1998, also played that year for the Kingdom.

How did Keenan convince Franklin, a resident of Arlington, Virginia, to play in Michigan for a summer? "Good recruiting," he said.

PDSL players cannot receive direct cash payment for playing, but Keenan gives each player free housing and a $100 monthly stipend for food. They also can work at 14 soccer camps the team organizes during the summer. If a player worked every camp, he could earn $1,300 per month. Most averaged about $600 per month.

In 1996 and 1997, the Kingdom averaged 2,200 fans per game. In 1998, that attendance fell to 2,000, but for good reason. The Kalamazoo Quest, a first year W-League franchise also owned by the Keenans, averaged about 500 spectators per game. Ticket prices are $3 presold and $5 at the gate.

The Keenans have built a solid franchise with an approach that stresses good business ahead of winning. "My big belief is that the finances should be as important, if not more important, than winning," said Keenan, who is the team's president and, for the first time next season, will be the head coach. "A lot of teams go into something like this and fold because they care more about winning."

The Kingdom and Quest are a livelihood for Keenan, 32, and Stephanie, 30, the team's director of marketing and business manager. Keenan credits strong community support for the success of his USISL franchises. They have even started a youth program that includes 240 players aged U-13 to U-19. Each year three players from the youth program graduate to the Kingdom's roster.

"This is all we do," said Chris Keenan. "We pay ourselves a middle-class wage. It's good enough to have two cars, go on a yearly vacation and pay a mortgage on a house. We're doing okay. I can show anybody how to make a small fortune in soccer. Take a large fortune, invest in soccer and it will become a small fortune."

The Keenans are content with keeping their soccer kingdom right where it is. "I'm not interested in playing D3, but I'd love to think that one day we could be in the A-League. But if I went to the A-League, I would have to put a worse product on the field."

One team trying their hand at D3 is the Royals. They've entered a market that appeals strongly to Marcos. "It's important because the amount of soccer in Northern Virginia is incredible," he said. "Between the soccer moms and their kids, and the Latinos, this is a market that should get up to 2,000 people (per game) if the right work is done and (the owners) have the means to stay the course."

Will Marcos stay the course with the USISL? He has a two-year agreement with Umbro that gives them an option to buy him out at the end of the term.

"They could say 'maybe you should stay on as chairman of the board and direct it philosophically, and let somebody else spend the next ten years with renewed energy (on) another phase," he said. "I want to be able to see this country populated with green grass inside little stadiums. I want to be able to leave it knowing that (the league) is going to stay here forever and that it is contributing significantly to the sport in this country at all levels."

THINK 13

My job as a publisher and writer offered some freedom to work varying hours. I am not married and was not involved in a restrictive romantic relationship. I enjoy all the elements of playing soccer—the aerobic and anaerobic training, the slightly acrobatic and completely artful skills required, the camaraderie of a compatible team and the smell and feel of fresh grass under the boots, to name just a few. Ever since I was a knee-knocking and hyperactive kid, I had wanted to be a professional athlete.

Why not, then, spend portions of my 39th spring and 40th summer—just short of five months in all—to train with and document the efforts of a new team in the lowest level of professional soccer in the U.S., for no immediate money and little, if any, immediate recognition?

About a decade ago, when I had just launched a precarious career as a full time free-lance writer, I had an idea that never became reality. I wanted to write about trying out for the Professional Golf Association Tour by playing in its qualifying school, a grueling test considered one of the mentally toughest in sports.

I wrote a note to George Plimpton and asked for advice. Plimpton, now one of the most respected writers and editors in the world, in the mid

1960s penned *Paper Lion*, his first-person account of playing quarterback for the Detroit Lions despite never before having played organized football. I read the book when I was a pre-teen and was immediately intrigued about the concept of documenting a personal effort to play professional sports.

This was back when Nike had just ballooned onto the sports apparel scene with its now famous motto.

Plimpton wrote back a note that said, simply, "Just do it."

Finally, I have done it, albeit in a different sport.

It took awhile for the author (No. 21), shown during a practice in April, to feel comfortable with his teammates.

I've been blessed with a gratifying past of varied athletic participation, success and disappointment. Country club sports—golf, tennis and swimming—along with basketball, dominated my competitive adolescent period. I grew up with three brothers born within four years of each other. We always had enough players for a backyard game of touch football, basketball or a variety of baseball games (soccer came later, when I entered high school). In his prime, my father was a semi-pro baseball player, a national-class sprinter and a near-scratch golfer. It was easy to develop a competitive spirit in that environment.

By the time I reached my mid teens, I was breaking 80 on the golf course almost as often as I tossed clubs in the air or against the ground out of anger and frustration. The game and my temperament did not mix.

Soccer and track reaped many rewards while at Notre Dame High School in Trenton, New Jersey. The Fighting Irish soccer team won the New Jersey state Catholic titles my junior and senior years, during which time I was elected all-state as a forward. After missing most of my junior year of track due to injury, I won the county title and finished fifth in the state and second in the Eastern States championships in the 800 meters during my senior year.

The author hoped collegiate track habits of 20 years ago would help make fitness sessions a little easier at practice.

I progressed to the University of Maryland, where I received a track scholarship and made the soccer team my freshman year. My college soccer career was regrettably brief. I strained an Achilles tendon during a training run prior to a preseason scrimmage. I was slated to start for the first time in that game, at outside forward. In the previous scrimmage, against Catonsville Community College near Baltimore, I scored a goal from a corner kick.

That would be my only collegiate soccer score. My track coach, who was paying my scholarship, said I could no longer play soccer due to the injury, which prevented me from running for four months.

Track was equally as frustrating. I compiled just one injury-free year, during my junior season. That year, I ran a personal best of 1:49.7 in the 800 meters, but missed qualifying for the national championships by seven tenths of a second. I missed the entire outdoor season, the same year of the 1980 Olympic Track and Field Trials, due to an ankle tendon injury. I had to improve my time by about one second to qualify for the trials.

Continuous physical discomfort plagued me during my 20s. A lower back problem blossomed when I was 24 after my back went into spasm at work as I bent down to pick up an envelope.

It was determined that I have a congenital disorder that causes my lower vertebrae to slowly degenerate.

Once I recovered, I tried feebly to continue a running career, but suffered repeated setbacks from strained calf muscles and lower back pain. During the 1980s I ran primarily for fitness rather than competition.

After I started regular treatments with a chiropractor in the late 1980s, and made some minor adjustments to my lifestyle, my full health slowly returned. I started wearing orthotics, specially fitted inserts for shoes. The chiropractor determined that my left leg is 3 millimeters shorter than the right. Orthotics solved that problem. I stopped sleeping on my stomach, relieving the pressure on my lower back. I bent at the knees instead of forward at the hips when I picked objects up off the floor.

I did not play soccer for some 15 years. In 1991, a former Maryland soccer teammate told me about pick-up games held each Saturday morning at a recreational field on the Maryland campus in College Park. The games originated in the mid 1960s near the time the University of Maryland was a co-national collegiate soccer champion.

My play the first day back surely provided comedy for, and prompted concern from, the other players—comedy for my dwindled skills and concern that I would hurt someone or get hurt myself.

I ran around recklessly with abandonment and the awkwardness of a newly-born colt. Still, I thoroughly enjoyed running the soccer field again and the environment, especially the post-game beers we consumed.

The mix of players intrigued me and the simplicity of the arrangement attracted me. Ranging in age from 15 to 75, many of the players had developed their skills in foreign lands—a Brazilian and a Brit, both in their 70s; a Frenchman and a German in their 50s; players in their 30s and 40s from Cameroon, Ghana, and the Caribbean.

Most were Americans, including several former University of Maryland teammates. One player, Donnie Kraft, joined his dad on the field, an honor most fathers and sons would cherish. I ultimately learned that Donnie's father, Ernie—now in his 60s—was born and raised in my hometown of Trenton, New Jersey. Ernie was a big fan of my dad and often talked with glee about how my dad's heralded baseball and track exploits prompted his continuous admiration while a youth.

Although played as "friendlies"—games with no league or tournament significance—inherent approaches to the game often provoked irrational passion. Some of the calmer and friendlier players off the field exhibited barbaric behavior on the field. One time a son of a French diplomat chased another player off the field with a large rock in his hand. The scene was comical—pursuee avoiding pursuer with a slanting and cutting route through players standing bewildered on the pitch—but also pathetic.

Players called fouls too often fueled by emotion rather than practical judiciousness. Arguments prevailed weekly and at times resulted in a punch or two being thrown. When you consider the multinational personalities involved, I was surprised all-out brawls did not erupt.

In at least one case, history seemed the catalyst for continuous animosity between two players. Some French natives still harbor resentment toward the Germans for Hitler's obliteration of France during World War II. Many of us figured that was the main reason two men in their 50s— Mark, a Frenchman and Gunther, a German—squared off almost weekly in verbal battles often laced with blood-boiling hostility.

Despite the disparities, the group has been largely chummy through the seven years I've been playing. The camaraderie was most evident after the games, when the beer started flowing at a nearby parking lot or at a local pizza and beer joint amid deep discussions that reflected the worldly differences of the group's varied cultures.

Within a year of playing in the pick-up games, a strong yearning to play organized soccer had returned. From 1992 to 1994, I played in over-30 and open men's leagues in Howard County, Maryland and in downtown Washington, D.C.

In 1995, I called a friend and coach to help me find a team to play on in Northern Virginia. Pete England had prominently coached youth teams, primarily the VISTA Blackwatch, to respectability in the Washington area and to the U. S. Youth Soccer National Championships in 1994. He was assembling a new team composed mostly of members of his youth teams in the Northern Virginia Soccer League (NVSL) and asked me to try out for the team.

The NVSL is comprised of four divisions and composed mostly of former college players in their early and mid 20s. I was 36. I felt honored and excited that England asked me to play. Cynically, I thought that England, a consummate but good-natured ballbuster, might get a kick out of me performing inadequately against them.

His NVSL team included mostly players in their late teens who England wanted to toughen up against some older opponents in preparation for the national youth tournament. When I tried out for the team in a practice game one early spring evening, I was nearly twice as old as most of the players on the team. But rather than feeling old, I actually felt invigorated to be on the field with a bunch of youngsters.

While I did not expect to match skill level with the other players, I was confident my fitness would easily carry me through the game. I ran regularly—a mixture of easy distance runs up to five miles, quicker distance runs up to three miles, and fartleks (intervals incorporated into a short distance run)—lifted weights a couple of days a week for upper body strength and played hard pick-up games regularly on Saturday mornings during the off-season.

My goal was to keep it simple—hustle on the flanks, make some hard runs to the corners, play aggressive defense and send in some effective crosses to the center of the field.

I felt I played a solid match. Coach England concurred. He said after the game, with a little touch of surprise in his tone, that he was impressed, and that I should join them for their league match the following weekend.

Coach England and I later enjoyed a couple of post-game beers—a luxury he could not enjoy with his other players. Was that the real motivation for asking me to try out for his team? Maybe he just wanted another drinking buddy. I could easily fulfill that role.

The biggest problem with drinking a couple of beers after a game is that you often sit down during consumption. That is normally not a problem for a young player. But when you reach your late-30s, the muscles tend to stiffen a bit, especially if you've injured one of them.

Toward the middle of my 45 minutes or so of playing time, I tried to send a long ball out of the defensive midfield. I leaned a bit too far back on my planted left leg, as I kicked the ball with my right leg, and felt a little pop. I strained a tendon that connected the quadriceps muscle to the knee. It felt fine unless I needed to support myself while leaning back. Some stopping and pivoting moves were uncomfortable. But the injury was not crippling.

As I walked out of the bar, the injury had swelled and the muscle felt as stiff as a double shot of bourbon. I thought there was no way I could play in the team's first league match a few days later and, further, that my days as a Blackwatch player had ended after one practice game.

Coach England laughed at me as I limped to my car. Laugh at me, will you? I had to show him I could play.

I played that first game and finished the spring season hampered a bit by the injury. Playing with the younger players proved to be a real test of physical conditioning. Fortunately, the injury did not prevent me from my training runs and light soccer drills during the week, so I was able to maintain a strong level of fitness.

Still, I realized I needed to adjust my training if I hoped to play effectively against the younger players. My game was predicated on a lot of running and hustle. I left the finesse stuff to the better-skilled players.

So after that season, I decided to alter my preseason conditioning.

On advice from a close friend who had been a conditioning coach for the New Jersey Nets of the National Basketball Association, I instituted more strength exercises for my legs. Up until that time, I had avoided weight-assisted strength training for my legs, thinking if it was done improperly I could create muscle imbalances, which would increase the chance of injury.

The coach, Rich Snedaker, boasted to me that he had made Nets superstar forward Jayson Williams into one of the strongest players in the NBA. I figured if it worked for Jayson, it would work for me.

Snedaker suggested I start two months before the season with three exercises two to three times a week: standing squats on a Smith machine with light weight; lunges with barbells in my hands; and seated squats. He suggested the Smith machine for the standing squats because the bar is connected to vertical supports that help control the movement better. And it was safer than using a free-standing bar.

A consistent program yielded tremendous results. I felt greatly improved leg strength on the field and during my training runs. It felt easier to kick long balls and my shots developed more zip. Most importantly, the recovery time for my legs had been cut in half. Reduced recovery time permits accelerated training. The work paid off. I stayed injury-free the next two years.

The next adjustment was playing alongside a bunch of fun high school kids. I consider myself less mature than most people my age. And most of my friends will attest to that. But trying to relate to my high-school-aged Blackwatch teammates on any kind of intellectual level was like preaching a 12-step program to a devoted wino. After a while, you give up, let them be and just enjoy their company.

During times of personal doubt when I thought I should grow up — thankfully, those moments were rare — I would go to a game or practice and be thrown right back into the depths of juvenile jocularity.

I must admit at times it was refreshing. Instead of talking about work or family — which most of my peers did — my Blackwatch mates babbled mostly about typical teen-age problems — dating, favorite television shows, where the next party was, sex, and how much beer they drank.

Most of them didn't work. They used the word "dude" a lot. They cared little about foreign policy or reductions in the federal budget. On weekends, they liked to stay out real late and wake up when most of my friends began their afternoon naps.

That transformed the beginning of our 9 a.m. and 11 a.m. Sunday games into groan fests. While most of our opponents arrived chipper and ready to play, some of the younger Blackwatch boys arrived at the field groggy and hung over.

Meanwhile, I tried to be at the field one hour before the game to ensure that I was fully flexed, stretched and adrenalized by game time. I was amazed at how most of my teammates could show up 10 minutes before a game, lace up their boots and start running hard from the game's outset.

Sometimes, when you are young, your priorities are really screwed up. We had to forfeit one spring season game because of a high school prom. I repeat — A HIGH SCHOOL PROM. If a team does not have eight players by game time, they are forced to forfeit the game. The night before, about half our team attended a prom. How dare they prefer a possibly romantic evening over a good night's sleep.

Two years after joining the Blackwatch, I was picked for the NVSL All-Star team for the fall 1997 season. Each league coach picked two players from their team. I was certain I was picked because I showed up for every game, not because I was one of the top two players on the team. And I was certain Coach England would not admit that, so I just accepted the appointment with little fanfare and much pride.

The best result of my playing time with the Blackwatch is that it has placed me in a young frame of mind. When you think young, you play young. But, sometimes you may also act younger than you should. My mother reminded me frequently—I stress she never nagged—that I should think more about acting my age. She preferred that I stop playing silly athletic games with kids half my age. Dad was more supportive. He offered simple advice to just do whatever I could.

I imagine that Carl Lewis would have supported my endeavor to play a sport at a highly competitive level at such an age. Lewis had become an inspiration to me after he appeared—once in person—on a couple of radio shows I hosted. Meeting him made his accomplishments more emphatic to me.

In his second book, *One More Victory Lap*, Lewis wrote about a dilemma he faced as he got older. At the age of 34 Lewis was preparing for his final Olympic effort at the 1996 Summer Games in Atlanta, Georgia. His year before the Games was marred by injury and poor performance.

He knew he had to change the way he prepared, both mentally and physically, to improve his chances of winning one more Olympic Gold Medal. He drastically changed his diet and training routine. And he altered how he mentally approached his training.

Lewis had developed a strong mentor relationship with spiritual leader Sri Chinmoy. Sri Chinmoy is known for conquering, and helping to inspire others to conquer, fears and doubts to accomplish amazing athletic feats while promoting peace and serenity. He's Ghandi with stronger muscles.

The Sri Chinmoy 3,100-mile race takes place annually in the height of summer heat in Queens, New York. Six runners started the 1998 event in June, running up to 16 hours a day on a lap course through the streets of Queens. The winner completed the race in 50 days, a remarkable average of 62 miles per day.

Sri Chinmoy has registered some amazing feats as well. In October 1998, the 67-year-old, 145-pounder lifted a 200-pound dumbbell overhead nine times with one arm. Chinmoy's stated goal during the conquest was to demonstrate that "if we can develop inner strength and inner peace, then this world will have harmony and the feeling of oneness."

After his trying season and with the Olympics one year away, Lewis consulted with Sri Chinmoy, who often offered an eager ear and inspirational advice to the greatest sprinter who ever lived. In part, Chinmoy told Lewis to imagine that he was 13.

"You have to forget about your age," Sri Chinmoy tells Lewis in the book. "Be 13. Always think of this number, 13, and keep the energy and desire of someone who is 13. Then you will always be young. You will always run young."

Whenever Lewis felt doubt, he said to himself, "13....13." He trained with renewed vigor and enriched wisdom. And at the 1996 Summer Olympics, he won the long jump to earn his ninth Gold Medal, tying three other athletes for the most Olympic gold medals ever won.

My goal was drastically more simple than Lewis's. I wanted to complete a full season with the Royals without suffering a serious injury. And I hoped to play in just one game. During my quest, which began in early April, I thought often about the number 13.

Suddenly, the number 13 felt quite lucky.

ROAD RAGE

The cheerful and affable Silvino Gonzalo portrays a pleasant personality. He jokes with his players, encourages them sincerely during practice and games and evokes a comfortable sense of humor. Towards the end of the team's second game, a horrid 4-0 loss to the Western Massachusetts Pioneers, the Royals set up for a corner kick as the closing seconds ticked off the clock. A frustrated fan, hoping to encourage a late score, suddenly yelled out, "Quick, the goalie's down."

Many of the barely 500 spectators attending the match laughed quietly, but their collective chuckle echoed clearly to the bench. Grim-faced most of the match, Gonzalo turned toward the crowd and mustered an appreciative smile, perhaps thanking the small faithful for the bit of comic relief amid a miserable day.

It is this likability that has endeared Gonzalo to many of the Royals players and convinced them to make a commitment to the team, despite the fact they do not get paid.

At times, though, during a practice or game, the Royals coach can explode into brief profanity-laden flurries of anger. Gonzalo can send a strong message when he feels the need.

When he addressed the team at the end of practice before their first road trip to face the Reading (Pennsylvania) Rage, he firmly told them that the bus would leave at 1 p.m. and tagged his statement with a warning.

"If you are not there, you do not go," he said firmly.

Everyone seemed to absorb the message.

But how many athletes have listened cynically to such a warning from a coach? Probably thousands. Would the coach really leave if one of the best players was a few minutes late?

In most cases, no. But I was part of one situation that showed no tolerance by our coach. During my first year of playing varsity soccer in high school, I made a last-minute stop to the bathroom before boarding a team bus, a result of an on-rushing bowel movement prompted by typical pregame nerves. We were headed to a school about 30 minutes away for an early-season game. When I rushed out to the school parking lot to board the bus, I noticed it had left without me.

Slightly panicked, since I had just become a starter as a junior and I did not want to lose that position, I scurried about to find a ride to the game. Ironically, I found one from the girlfriend of the player I had replaced on the starting unit. She was quite the sport considering I was the reason her boyfriend was sitting on the bench and in a generally foul mood. I arrived at the field right at game time and was benched until the second half.

I expected at least one Royals player to arrive late for the departure to Reading.

A surprise greeted the Royals players, coaches and staff on May 1 as they pulled into the rendezvous point, a hotel parking lot near Tysons Corner in Northern Virginia. The team had initially planned to take a bus that would include some team supporters. For $15, each fan would receive the bus ride and a ticket to the game. But team management could not develop the promotion in proper time and canceled the idea.

It was purely a matter of economic sensibility. Taking the bus would have cost $3 a mile for a trip that covered about 400 miles up and back. Management decided instead to rent three vans for $65 a day, including mileage. The move saved the Royals about $800.

Still, riding in vans concerned Gonzalo.

"I don't like this. This is not good," he said, standing near one of the vans as his players slowly started to gather.

Certainly, any coach prefers a team bus to several smaller vehicles. A bus is more comfortable. Players can leave their seats and stretch their legs, a fairly important factor when playing a game several hours later. Further, everyone traveling on the same vehicle promotes team unity. It was still a young season for a first-year team and some players admittedly did not even know the last names of other players. And veteran athletes of bus trips know it is much easier to take naps on a bus than in a cramped van.

Finally, it is easier to control the actions of the players when they're not dispatched in separate vehicles. I speak from experience.

To cut costs, the track team at the University of Maryland occasionally traveled in station wagons or sedans provided by the state. This allowed a certain amount of freedom for the athletes, many of whom drove the cars themselves. The coaches allowed even more flexibility on return trips. During one ride back from an indoor meet at the University of Pittsburgh my senior year, we purposefully lagged behind the caravan to make it easier to buy beers for the ride.

Some four hours later, we pulled into the parking lot near the track office to drop off some of the athletes. Perhaps clouded by slight inebriation and fatigue, I foolishly decided to dump the empty beer bottles into a dumpster I assumed was full of other debris. I figured it was best to ditch the evidence as soon as possible.

The beer bottles landed on the bottom of the empty dumpster with a resounding crash that sounded like a chandelier had fallen from the sky. Within seconds, an assistant coach walked out of the track office wondering which nucklehead had created such an irresponsible disturbance.

The coach did not yell or rave. He simply told me that I had done a stupid thing, certainly an action not expected of the team captain. He threatened to strip me of that role. I felt humiliated and embarrassed. I retained the captaincy, but the several days of uncertainty proved ample punishment for the misdeed.

Granted, the Royals players were all beyond college age and presumably more mature. Besides, the team would spend the night in Reading and return the next morning. If the coach worried about a van wandering off to gather beer for the ride home in the morning, perhaps he should hire a team psychologist.

All but two players had met the 1 p.m. deadline. It was time for Gonzalo to lay down the law or exercise a little leniency. He opted for the latter, perhaps because the late players were star right back Chris Jones and the other was reserve keeper Andrew Scogna. It would be tough to play one of the top teams in the league without your best marking back and with just one keeper.

So he pushed back the cut-off time.

"We wait until ten after one and then we leave," the slightly annoyed Gonzalo said. Meanwhile, the other players took the situation in stride. They showed no discomfort in the delay and sat calmly in the vans waiting for their teammates to appear.

Scogna and Jones pulled into the parking lot right at 1:10 p.m. By the end of the trip, Jones might have wished he had stayed home.

The Royals headed north having lost their last two games and hours away from facing last season's Mid-Atlantic division winner. After winning the home opener, the Royals lost 4-0 at home to the Pioneers and then 1-0 to the Delaware Wizards. In the loss to the Wizards, the much awaited debut of forward Rachid Mahboub, a 23-year-old Moroccan, ended unimpressively after beginning with much promise.

By the time he joined the Royals, Mahboub had already proven himself as a top player in Morocco. He was a member of the U-15 and U-20 Moroccan National Teams. At age 19, Mahboub joined the Wydad Athletic Club's elite team in the Moroccan National League's top division and scored half a dozen goals in a year and a half as a central forward.

Mahboub signed with Wydad for a $15,000 bonus and made $500 per win and $350 per tie. He earned no money if the team lost.

Mahboub used about a third of that signing bonus to finance his stay in the United States, which he first visited during the 1994 World Cup. He gave the rest of the money to his father, whose export/import business had declared bankruptcy. The money helped Mahboub's father retain his business.

Despite his relative comfort as a well-paid professional soccer player in Morocco, Mahboub was lured to the U.S. for "its different lifestyle, its freedom," he said. "But I made the wrong decision. It was stupid. I was playing full time, practicing every day and traveling. But when you're in a third world country, if you go to a great country (like the U.S.), you think you will have more options and better opportunities."

Mahboub arrived in the U.S. alone. He sought a professional soccer career in the U.S. and took English classes at Northern Virginia Community College. "That first year I was just chilling and spending my money and going to school," he said.

When he could stay on the field, Rachid Mahboub showed flashes of offensive brilliance.

Mahboub continued his soccer career playing for two semi-professional teams in the Washington area, the Washington Athletic Club in a Moroccan League and River Plate, a Spanish team in an international league in Virginia. His fees for those teams ranged from $80 to $150 a game.

But Mahboub's savings eventually ran out and in 1996 he took a job as a full-time waiter at Tuscana West, an Italian Restaurant in downtown Washington, D.C. Once he joined the Royals, many times he worked a day shift—on his feet for six to eight hours—before he practiced with the team at night.

Mahboub, a polite and congenial man, possesses the skills and strength to play at the MLS level. He nearly made it to the MLS combine in 1995. That fall he advanced through a weekend of MLS tryouts in the Washington, D.C. area before being cut in the last round.

In 1996, Mahboub was offered a full scholarship to play at The University of Kentucky after the school's coach saw him play in Atlanta with River Plate at an indoor tournament. Mahboub accepted the offer, but he returned to the Washington area after four weeks to support his sisters, who had just moved to the U.S. and were living in his apartment.

"I felt disappointed, but I couldn't leave my sisters alone," he said.

In the fall of 1997, a friend of Mahboub's called Royals owner Mo

Sheta to watch him play at an indoor tournament in Manassas, Virginia. But Mahboub missed the tournament after he was called in to work at the last minute. Sheta finally saw Mahboub play during a Royals tryout in January 1998.

When Mahboub signed a three-year contract with the Royals the following March, he knew he would not make money. "They asked me if I can help them out the first year, and if they had something to pay later, they would pay me," he said. "I like Mo (Sheta). He's a nice guy. He's very diplomatic and he respects people. And he's a funny guy. We're both Arab so it's not hard for us to communicate."

Mahboub, a big and aggressive forward with a solid shot and refined finesse, showed the first time he touched the ball in the Wizards game why he can be so dangerous.

He made a crafty run from near midfield towards the right corner before serving a threatening cross into the box.

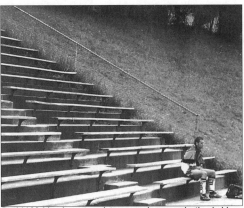

Rachid Mahboub contemplates an early game ejection in his first appearance with the Royals.

Minutes later, he launched a rocket from just outside the 18-yard line that landed with a muffled thud as the goalkeeper caught it against his chest.

But Mahboub was off the field some 20 minutes into the match. While tracking back to chase a Wizards defender dribbling out of their own box, he profoundly and illegally tackled the player from behind with a loud whack that sounded like bone against bone. The defender was miraculously uninjured, and Mahboub was shown the red card.

Mahboub spent the rest of the match sitting in the bleachers, much of the time in solemn solitude in a far corner of the front row.

When the Royals traveled five days later to Reading, they faced a team that was staging its home opener. And the Rage can put on a good show.

In 1996, the Rage's first season in the league, the USISL voted them as the league's top organization. They averaged around 1,500 fans a game their first year and spectator interest remained strong in 1997.

Rage management, anticipating a continuous crowd increase, moved their games in 1998 to a high school field that accommodated 3,600 spectators. Continuous rain kept the home opener crowd to several hundred, but the atmosphere reflected the passion the team's fans and management pour forth for the Rage.

About 15 minutes before game time, a white stretch limousine drove into the stadium as the public address system blared upbeat music.

As the vehicle stopped behind the team benches, the public address announcer urged the crowd to welcome a "V.I.B."-"Very Important Bull."

When the Royals made their first road trip to Reading, starter Jan Da Weer, right, had already left the team, leaving John Pascarella, left, as the No. 1 goalkeeper.

On cue, "Rage," the team mascot dressed in a radiant red bull outfit, trotted out on the field to spark some enthusiasm in the crowd. A few minutes later, each Rage player, escorted by a youth player from the area, ran onto the field as they were introduced and passed by "Rage," who offered a quick pat on the back or slap handshake.

Throughout the game, "Rage" frolicked with the saturated crowd, eliciting cheers and guffaws from the younger demographic.

The home team played more like a distressed deer—tentative, confused, indifferent—than a raging bull in the first half. Their defense was extremely disorganized in the first 15 minutes and allowed its first goal in the third minute. From about six yards out, striker Tony Trepal punched in a loose ball in front of the goal that was crossed in from the right side. And the Royals missed a couple more golden scoring chances during that time.

Mahboub started at forward for the second consecutive game for the Royals, replacing the suddenly uninvolved Scott Poirier. Gonzalo explained at half time why Poirier sat on the bench. "I like Scott, he's a good player," he said. "But he's not in good shape. It would be tough for him tonight in these tough conditions. He can not play two games in three days. Plus, Rachid can not play Sunday."

Mahboub was able to play following a game in which he received a red card due to a quirky league rule. A player receiving a red card can not play in the next game seven days after receiving the card. This allows ample time for a full review in the case of an appeal. The Reading game was five days after Mahboub took the red card. He would have to sit out the Royals next game two days later.

The feisty Moroccan seemed intent on earning a reputation as the "player to receive most bookings per minute." He received a yellow card in the 8th minute for faking an injury, giving him two cards in his first 25 minutes of play for the Royals.

A glaring omission for the Royals was Jan Da Weer, who commanded the goal well in the team's opener. Since then, John Pascarella had started in the two losses.

At the end of the final practice before the trip, Da Weer announced that he was moving to his hometown of St. Louis. Da Weer had accepted a job as a manager at a sporting goods store. The announcement seemed to catch the team by surprise.

After Da Weer's announcement, as most players walked away from the practice field in the fading twilight of a pleasant spring evening, Da Weer lingered to help Pascarella practice some final drills. Lying on the ground off to the side of the field, Pascarella rolled from one side to the other as Da Weer tossed balls far enough to make Pascarella stretch to corral them. The lights from a nearby car provided sufficient illumination for the two to continue their routine. Pascarella's ambition seemed bred from the opportunity to return to the starting lineup.

Pascarella helped keep the Rage scoreless in the first half, but his netminding created concern during a heated half time locker room session. The point of hottest contention dealt with a communication problem in the backfield. A couple of defenders, most vehemently Chris Jones, asked Pascarella to declare his intentions when he came off his line to thwart an offensive push by the Rage. A couple of times Gonzalo had to calm the players.

But Pascarella adamantly defended his silent aggression, saying that it's best he does not vocally warn the defenders he's coming out of goal when the ball is on the ground "because their heads are down." Pascarella sought the element of surprise.

Steady Steve Gill ended the half time session with an upbeat oration.

"We get one more goal and they're dead," he said. "If we don't get one first, keep your heads up. We will get another one."

It didn't take long for the Rage to take control of the second half. Aided in part by moving a midfielder forward, creating a three-man front line, the Rage scored three unanswered goals in the first 25 minutes of the second half.

By the time midfielder Rick Engelfried received a red card with his team down 2-1, the rains had become torrential and seemed to wash away any hopes of the Royals to stage a comeback.

It seemed inevitable that the Rage would ultimately dominate the game. They returned nine starters from last year's Mid-Atlantic division championship team, including Ian Hennessy, a 31-year-old sweeper who played for the MetroStars in Major League Soccer's inaugural season.

It was the first game of the season for the Rage, and after the game coach Paul Moylan said he was not surprised at his team's poor first half performance.

"We came out tentative," he said. "The guys are still not used to each other."

He then flashed a sly smile. "I've always wanted to say this," he said. "The first half was even. And the second half was even worse."

There was no jocularity in the Royals locker room. After the game, the ill feelings that brewed between Jones and Pascarella at half time rose to a breaking point. Soon after entering the locker room, Pascarella started throwing things and cursing randomly.

"Now's not the time to be mad. It's time to be mad on the field," said Jones. The two then screamed at each other and were separated by teammates before the hostility turned violent.

After tempers cooled, Gonzalo tagged his post-game talk with a sincere ultimatum. "If we don't win Sunday, there will be some changes," he said. "Think about it, guys."

As Gonzalo walked quietly away from his players, he passed a glum-faced Jones, sitting on a bench and staring into space.

A little later, while Jones showered, Pascarella and team owner Mo Sheta engaged in a visceral shouting match. Pascarella was unhappy that towels for taking a shower arrived late into the locker room. "I thought they were going to rip each other's face off," said Jones.

The team spent the night at a nearby hotel rather than drive back home immediately following the game. Gonzalo wanted his players to get a good night's rest. Their next game commenced in Northern Virginia in 40 hours.

Chris Jones sat on a stool in the middle of the second floor bar, surrounded by a small flock of happy D.C. United fans, many of them with a mild, happy-go-lucky, alcoholic buzz. The defending Major League Soccer champions had handily beaten the Chicago Fire, 4-1, on this mid-July, Saturday afternoon. The team had gathered in downtown Washington, D.C. with its most loyal supporters at The Rock, a rusticly-chic sports bar across the street from the MCI Center, to bask in a post-victory glow.

Jones soaked up the scene with his characteristic broad smile and illuminated expression hiding severe fatigue. It had been a hectic two days of combining hobby (playing for the Royals) and vocation (Mid-Atlantic Representative for adidas).

"Man, I am wiped," he said with a look of contentment.

He then explained his whirlwind last 24 hours: playing for the Royals the night before in Myrtle Beach, South Carolina; driving a few hours with John Pascarella to Raleigh, North Carolina, where they captured a few hours sleep; then back on the road by 7 a.m. to return to RFK Stadium in time to host an adidas party prior to the D.C. United game.

He lamented about his lack of fitness since he had been practicing sparingly with the Royals due to a hectic work-travel schedule.

"I'm getting through games on adrenaline," he said.

When fully fit, Jones promotes an imposing and dangerous combination of speed and finesse on the field. A tall, muscular and thin defender, Jones was an All-South Atlantic Region pick his senior year at Georgetown

University in 1994. That year, Jones scored two goals for the Hoyas in its first round match in the National Collegiate Athletic Association tournament, which they lost to the University of Maryland, 4-3 in overtime.

He played for the former Washington Mustangs of the USISL his first summer out of college and then joined the indoor Tampa Bay Terror in the National Professional Soccer League the following fall. Jones was not paid by either team.

Chris Jones tried to balance a pro soccer career with a professional promotional career with adidas.

Jones, who grew up in Trenton, New Jersey, returned to Washington in December 1995 for an open tryout staged by Major League Soccer. It was one of nine open tryouts that attracted several thousand players hoping to be among the 250 that would be selected for a league scouting combine the next month.

About 350 attended the Washington area tryout at George Mason University. A cool, overcast day greeted the pro wannabes. They were given numbers, selected to a team and then herded to one of four fields to play a series of 10-minute, small-sided games. About a dozen players were picked from each field to play in two full-field games in the afternoon. A couple dozen more would be picked from the afternoon game to play another game the next morning at Georgetown University. A final few would be selected from that game to attend the combine.

Jones played all the way through to the final game at his alma mater, but he was not selected for the combine. "I was pretty disenchanted," he said. "I walked away from the game for awhile."

While working as the Soccer Director for D.C. Scores, an inner-city soccer and mentoring program that works with Washington, D.C. public schools, Jones started playing soccer again. A close friend who played for Rutgers University, Tony Zea, was playing for Iberia, one of the top amateur teams in the Washington, D.C. area. Zea persuaded Jones to attend an Iberia practice and Jones joined the team soon after.

Iberia's coach was Gonzalo. He and Jones ultimately developed not only a close and successful player-coach relationship but also a strong friendship. Jones joined the team shortly after they won the 1996 U.S. National Men's Amateur Cup. In 1997, Jones and Royals teammates Alberto Ogando, Matt Ferry, Leonardo Thiombiano, Devin Payton and Mark Vita were part of the Virginia State team that won the Region I (Mid-Atlantic and Northeast) tournament and finished second at the prestigious Donnelly Cup. Also in 1997, Jones and Ferry played for the Region I amateur all-star team that won the Olympic Festival.

Jones' stellar play at the Donnelly Cup persuaded Tampa Bay Mutiny Coach John Kowalski to invite him to the team's preseason camp. Jones had already made a verbal commitment to play for the Jacksonville Cyclones of the A-League. But he faced a difficult decision. Jones was offered a job with adidas. He decided to refuse both the Mutiny's and the Cyclones's offers and accept the adidas job. Since D.C. United is one of his biggest clients, his office is housed at the team's practice facility in Herndon, Virginia.

Jones was wary of the uncertainty of making the Mutiny. "They were running a lot of players through camp," he said. " I went through that before (the MLS tryout in 1995) and did not want to go through that again."

The impending formation of the Royals certainly influenced Jones's decision to stay in D.C. It allowed him to compete in soccer at a high level, as he desired, and still hold an ideal job with one of the more successful and storied soccer equipment manufacturers in the world.

"I just want to play at the highest level I can," he said. "I don't want to do it for a living anymore. For me to play MLS, it would have to be the right opportunity. But I couldn't even tell you what that is because I haven't even thought about it."

Perhaps Jones thought more about the relative luxury of an MLS career as he endured the long drives to preseason practices two or three nights a week. The Royals practiced indoors at the Total Sports Pavilion. It took Jones about an hour to drive to practice, which began at 9 p.m. For the first month and a half, the team worked out, mostly on fitness, until midnight.

"We played with too many people on a surface that was rough on the body," he said. "But it was good in a sense that guys got to know each other well."

Jones had been working at United Park for about a month before practices began. He soon discovered glaring disparities in how an MLS team is organized compared to a USISL team. And Jones's discomfort with the Royals' way of doing things grew as the differences became more apparent.

"When we started, I felt like I was put into a leadership role because of my relationship with Silvino," he said in May. "But I wasn't happy with how some things were handled early on. So I stepped back from that role so I would not be too frustrated. Not being captain allows me to stay away from that a little bit.

"I come from a work situation where you're used to organization. Things like practice schedules. We find out at the end of training when the next practice is. It's hard to plan things like that. It would be nice to get a roster with names and phone numbers on it. There are a lot of guys on this team that I don't even know their last names yet. There's a kind of professionalism that I would like to see. That's why I don't want to be captain. I'd be bitching about it too much."

Jones admits that his play was "average" during the first few games of the season. Still, he was euphoric after the season-opening win, telling a friend after the game that, "It was fun to be out there, working your butt off, sweating like crazy."

The fun yielded to frustration during the next three games, all losses. Jones was his typically vocal self during half time of the Reading game. He was most contentious with Pascarella as they discussed a solution for the communication problem in the backfield.

Jones explained his bemusement about Pascarella's approach to on-field communication. "A goalie has never said to me don't call out when coming out (to clear the ball)," he said. "Working at D.C. United, and sometimes being a part of training, I see how things are run. I'm not saying everything has to be first class, but it should be done in a professional manner. A lot of this has nothing to do with money. "

Jones and Pascarella talked after the locker room fracas. "I have nothing against John personally or the skill level he is at," he said. "As long as his attitude is fine, I don't care."

STUNG BY A NOR'EASTER

The relentless rain in late April and early May converted soccer fields in the Washington, D.C. area into spongy mini swamps. If there was one consolation, the rain allowed the Royals to have their pick of fields at their unofficial practice site in Avenel, Maryland. The Royals' practice field was one of three fields in a small athletic park. In mid-June, practices were moved to a larger, more accommodating and better-cared-for athletic complex that is part of Lewinsville Park in McLean, Virginia.

Most of the youth teams that used the fields in Avenel stayed away until the skies dried and the fields drained. Water drained poorly, so the players were forced to navigate dozens of puddles that formed on the widespread dirt portions of the field.

There's a funny thing about playing on a soggy field. The moisture made insignificant the bumpy terrain underneath, allowing for a more even roll of the ball. The water was the great smoother of the dirt-spotted soccer fields that are prevalent in the Washington, D.C. area, an over-saturated soccer market with an inadequate number of fields. Often the ball skipped off the water or ended abruptly in a puddle.

The pitch that best tolerated the water was the outfield of a baseball field that was part of the complex. It was slightly more elevated than the Royals' normal practice pitch, allowing for better drainage, and the grass was at a more consistent, comfortable length. Baseball is rarely played in the rain, so there was no one competing for the space.

Practices on wet fields actually evolved into fun sessions after we adjusted to it. Any avid soccer player knows the juvenile joy of a slide tackle gone astray. Sure, you hope to get a touch on the ball and disrupt an attack. But if you don't, the prolonged slide through the water creates pure elation for any player with a sense of adventure.

The rain, though, would mostly be no fun at all for the Royals. And it would contribute to its disheartening inaugural campaign.

I n times of need, a weakened warrior often seeks help from an older, wiser and more accomplished sibling. Fortunately for the Royals, family connections led directly to the most successful franchise in MLS's brief history. Big brother D.C. United would show the Royals the value of familial support.

Two days after the ruckus in Reading, the Royals earned a brave 1-0 overtime win over the Rhode Island Stingrays. The saviors for the Royals were Chris Jones and Mark Simpson, the goalkeeper who helped D.C. United win the first MLS Cup in 1996. D.C. United, the Royals' affiliate MLS team, loaned Simpson and defender Curt Onolfo to the Royals for that game.

MLS star Mark Simpson often filled the net for the Royals as he tried to recover from an injury that limited his playing time for D.C. United.

With Simpson in goal and Onolfo as stopper, Jones' comfort level in the backfield improved dramatically.

Simpson was the starting goalkeeper for D.C. United during most of its first championship season in 1996. But he played just seven games the following season because of a right knee injury. From June 23 to August 21, he endured three surgeries—to repair a torn Meniscus cartilage, to dissolve a subsequent and life-threatening infection and to remove scar tissue and loose bodies from the knee.

And it was much worse than that. Within a few days after the first surgery, Simpson's body temperature consistently rose over 101 degrees, he was vomiting regularly and his urine had turned orange.

"For 10 days after the surgery, I sweated through everything I wore at night and the bed sheets," he said.

The knee became infected. "Doctors have told me that the infection was caused by something going wrong in the care after the first surgery," he said.

The second surgery, ten days after the first, was intended to clean out the infection. The surgery saved his leg, but he lost 20 pounds in the next five days while sitting in a hospital bed consuming experimental antibiotics to find out which one could completely stop the lingering infection.

Immediately after the second surgery, Simpson was fitted with a PICC (Peripherally Inserted Central Catheter) line, a narrow tube inserted into a major vein in the arm that leads to the heart. The line allowed him to hook up more conveniently to an intravenous antibiotic, which he received three times a day for the next six weeks.

As soon as the antibiotic treatment ended, Simpson had his third surgery to remove scar tissue from the knee. "I didn't know how bad the knee was until the third surgery," he said. "I was told that if I had gone another week without the second surgery they probably would have amputated part of my leg."

While Simpson struggled to save his leg and his career, goalkeepers Scott Garlick and Tom Presthus helped lead D.C. United to another MLS title.

Simpson had hoped that the third surgery would allow him to rehabilitate his knee well enough for the 1998 season. But early in the season he discovered that an accumulation of more scar tissue prevented his knee from fully extending. D.C. United Head Coach Bruce Arena felt more confident with Garlick in goal and Presthus as his back-up to start off the season.

While Garlick and Presthus led United to another MLS Cup, Simpson spent most of 1998 on D.C. United's bench, playing in only two games. He trained regularly despite the less-than-fully rehabilitated knee. Simpson waited until after the 1998 season to have a fourth surgery on the knee, one that would finally, he hoped, remove any remaining scar tissue.

"I wanted to see how far I could come back," he said. "Then it made sense to wait until the end of the season, in case one of our keepers got injured."

Simpson had the surgery in late October 1998. "The infection ate out some of the Anterior Cruciate ligament, and the Meniscus cartilage," he said in early November 1998. "I've got more mobility now than I did before the surgery. A hamstring tendon was bothering me because I use that muscle to explode, but it was encased by the scar tissue."

Before the fourth surgery, Simpson's surgeon gave him a 50 percent chance of playing soccer again. Some 10 days after the surgery, Simpson — despite being waived from the team in late October — was talking about playing again for D.C. United in 1999.

While Simpson endured a trying season as United's third goalkeeper, he decided to play for the Royals so he could get some game time.

"I thought it was a good way for me to get back on the field," he said.

No other Royals player typified the soccer journeyman more than Simpson, a veteran of 10 years of professional soccer in the U.S. He played with five different indoor teams and two outdoor teams before joining D.C. United.

When he joined the Royals, he had experienced the small crowds that greet minor league teams. Simpson made his first appearance for the Royals against the Rhode Island Stingrays with only a couple hundred spectators in attendance. Against the Stingrays, Simpson made three game-saving plays, including one in the last five minutes, when he dashed off his line and thwarted a 1 v 1 chance about seven yards out. The Royals won 1-0 in overtime.

Following the debacle in Reading, Gonzalo had put the team on notice, saying that if they lost the game to Rhode Island, they would face some wholesale changes. Further, many players violated a team curfew after the Reading game by drinking alcoholic beverages into the wee hours of Saturday morning. Gonzalo warned the players at half time of the Stingrays game that if they did not win, they would practice Monday through Thursday the following week. He also said there would be bed checks after 11 p.m. on road trips.

Jones helped the team avoid a tough week of practice when he came up big with 57 seconds remaining in overtime in a scoreless game. Onolfo had sent in a restart that eluded the keeper in front of the goal. Jones swung at the ball about two yards from the goal line. The ball ricocheted back to Jones after hitting a player and he lifted the ball over two fallen players in front of him for the game winner.

"There was nothing pretty about it," he said.

There was little to admire about the team's effort that day as well, on and off the field. Gonzalo called it his team's worst performance of the young season.

Further, two players received red cards. Scott Poirier, who had entered the game with about 15 minutes remaining in regulation, was booked in overtime for a hard tackle from behind and was subsequently suspended for a surprising and harsh three games.

The passionate Pascarella continued to provide peripheral drama. He received a red card for dissension after yelling profanities at the referee from the bench during the game and had to leave the field. He received a two-game suspension. However unintended, the timing was perfect. Pascarella was leaving the team for 10 days and would miss their next three games to attend a West Coast wedding as a best man.

As the Royals prepared for their next three matches—all U.S. Open Cup qualifiers—they were clearly a disoriented team. They were tied with two other D3 teams, the Texas Toros and the Houston Hurricanes, for most red cards with four. Their goalkeeping situation was unsteady. Their play put their head coach on an emotional edge.

Gonzalo would have to suffer longer than expected. The next game— a home match against the New Hampshire Phantoms seven days after they beat the Stingrays—was canceled due to an unplayable field. Heavy rains saturated the poorly draining pitch. The Royals scheduled the game for eight days later, the only Monday playing date on the season's calendar.

Why a Monday? Pure practicality and part circumstance. The Royals were scheduled to play away games against Rhode Island (Saturday night), and the Cape Cod Crusaders (Sunday afternoon) the following week-end. Rescheduling the New Hampshire game for the next Monday made sense since the team would already be in New England for the weekend. And the Royals needed to complete all its preliminary U.S. Open Cup games by May 24th.

The U.S. Open Cup, the oldest annual tournament in U.S. sports history, is a national tournament open to all men's amateur and professional teams registered with the United States Soccer Federation. The Brooklyn Field Club won the first Cup in 1914. The Cup is based upon a similar tournament that was already established in England and most soccer-playing countries stage domestic open cup tournaments. D3 teams play round robin games in groups of several other D3 teams before advancing to single elimination play.

The Open Cup is a chance for the underdog teams to surprise heavily favored teams. One of those surprises almost happened in 1997. The San Francisco Bay Seals, a D3 team, advanced to the U.S. Open Cup semifinals, where they lost to D.C. United, the 1996 U.S. Open Cup champion and the two-time MLS champions.

The Royals would need a miracle to be the surprise team of the 1998 Open Cup. They were scheduled to play three games within 50 hours while on the road. The Royals were physically sound, but their psyche was slightly wounded. By the end of the trip—one that would be a defining moment for the Royals season—that decision to reschedule the rained out New Hampshire game seemed highly suspect. By the time the Royals limped home Monday night, a few key players suffered serious injuries. And their mental health was not much better.

T he Royals were relishing their brief bout with luxury. They sat slightly cramped but comfortable in their coach seats aboard a Southwest Airlines plane leaving Baltimore Washington International (BWI) Airport bound for Greene International Airport in Providence. They joked amongst themselves and chatted amiably with crew members. Perhaps they sensed, correctly, that this would be their only travel by plane all season.

Most of the camaraderie emanated from the back left section of the plane, where five players and Gonzalo sat in two rows of three facing each other. About a half-hour before the flight, Gonzalo had been somewhat stressed. He staged what was becoming a typical, mild, pre-trip anxiety attack. With the plane minutes from boarding, midfielder Adam Wilson had not yet arrived.

"I don't like this," said Gonzalo. "Somebody's going to get hurt and we're going to be short players." Wilson said later that he had set his alarm for 4:15 a.m. to meet some team members at 5:45 a.m. to ride together to the airport. His alarm clock sounded, but his girlfriend told him that he shut it right off and went back to sleep. Wilson awoke at 6:40, in Fairfax, Virginia. He needed to be at BWI-a good one hour drive in non-rush hour traffic-by 8 a.m. The flight departed at about 8:30.

Gonzalo relaxed when Wilson walked onto the plane after the other passengers had already boarded.

"Are you going to punish him?" asked a flight attendant jokingly, as she walked by Gonzalo.

"Can't say anything now," said Gonzalo, leaning into the aisle and flashing a suave smile. "We'll talk about it later."

From left, Silvino Gonzalo, Justin Kerns and Alberto Ogando relax on the plane ride that began their three-day trip to New England.

Later, while another flight attendant in the front of the plane reviewed pre-flight instructions, Gonzalo noticed his new friend not paying attention.

"You should be listening," he said, smiling, to the flight attendant. "You're setting a bad example."

Once off the ground, Gonzalo lamented about his team's tendency to accumulate red cards. Not only were Poirier and Pascarella unavailable for multiple games, but captain Rick Engelfried could not play in the first game of the road trip due to a red card he had received two games prior. Still, Engelfried made the trip to play in the last two games.

His strategy for three games in three days was simple.

"We will try to get an early goal and then lay back," he said. "We will play three defenders and five midfielders. Of our two forwards, one will be withdrawn to make overlaps for long balls. We want our outside midfielders to run to the corners."

Later that day, while lounging in his hotel room and relaxing at a restaurant near the hotel, Gonzalo reflected about his team and his coaching.

On that evening's game against Rhode Island: "I know they have a Scandinavian. We will put someone on him the entire game. And they have a Jamaican midfielder. We are concerned about him. You lose a good starter (Engelfried) and everything is so affected."

About team defense: "I hope we can do better marking, especially in the midfield. If we do, we can be the best in the league. You have to know when to mark and how to react. It's all mental. You can't teach that. Every game, I trust the players will do that."

More about the team's accumulated cards: "It is a difficult question because I was a temperamental player. I don't want to take that away from the players. I want them to be competitive. What bothers me is the stupid cards, like talking to the referees or tackling from behind."

About his approach to games: "I look at each game as a war. You go there to kill, to do battle. I worry about every game. If we have a good game today and have a victory, then I am not worried about tomorrow's game. If we lose tonight, then tomorrow will be a disaster."

Pierce Memorial Stadium in East Providence, Rhode Island, the home field of the Stingrays, has a comfortable feel that brings back thoughts of an era of simplistic soccer tradition.

Royals owner Mo Sheta marveled at the look and feel of the stadium as we walked the pitch while the players warmed up for the game. I had been practicing with the team for about six weeks but had not yet been considered for a game roster. I attended the trip purely as a writer.

"This is the kind of stadium I want to build in Northern Virginia," he said in a dreamy tone

The stadium, built in the mid 1930s and refurbished in the early 1990s, seats 8,000 spectators inside its white stone structure, on aluminum bleachers that run the full length of both touchlines.

Like most other stadiums the Royals would play in, the field is shared

The Royals pose for their first team photo before the Rhode Island game in New England. Front row, from left: Martin Brillantine, Justin Kerns, Maxx-Henry Frazier, Devin Payton, Alberto Ogando, Sean Lapier, Tony Trepal, Jeff Todd. Back row, from left: Rick Engelfried, Rachid Mahboub, Matt Ferry, Steve Gill, Jeff Standish, Chris Jones, Matt Wilson, Andrew Scogna.

by the football and soccer teams of a local high school. But no other stadium I saw had Pierce's quaint ambiance and the look similar to an old, small soccer park in a blue-collar town of England. Situated comfortably in a public park, the stadium appeared almost regal.

The Royals laid claim to the first triumph in what would be a grueling battle, scoring in the sixth minute when a limping and unmarked Tony Trepal, already hampered on an injured hamstring, ran onto a pass from Rachid Mahboub that rolled across the goal mouth. Trepal, who said before the game that the hamstring was about "80 percent," had just been cut down from behind.

A stocky and feisty striker, Trepal grew up in Springfield, Virginia and was a *Washington Post* All-Met and All-Region Selection at West Springfield High School his senior year. That year he was one of the top scorers in the Washington, D.C. area with 17 goals despite missing the last few games of the season with a knee injury.

He continued his scoring prowess at Division III Mary Washington

College in Fredericksburg, Virginia. Trepal tied a school record there for most goals in a season, scoring 20 his junior year.

Following college, Trepal played mostly amateur soccer with L.C.C., a rival of Iberia and Total Sports in the Northern Virginia Soccer League's Premier Division. Trepal later played for Gonzalo on the 1997 Virginia State team.

Before joining the Royals, Trepal yearned to see how far he could develop in professional soccer. He took part in an MLS tryout at George Mason University and left with a bad feeling after getting cut during the first day.

"I realized it was mostly who you knew," he said of the MLS tryout. "One of the reasons I joined the Royals was to get to know people."

Trepal had little trouble making the Royals. But he struggled throughout most of the season after he ripped a hamstring in practice after the third game. By that time he had secured a starting spot at forward. After the injury, he played at about 80 percent of full potential.

"I kept trying to play, but I kept missing scoring opportunities thinking I could do something when I couldn't," he said. "I really couldn't sprint or push off or cut."

Tony Trepal was an early season scoring leader for the Royals before an injury shortened his season.

Trepal scored two goals in the team's first six games. But his hamstring worsened after playing two of the three games during the road trip in New England. He failed to score another goal all season and sat out completely from early July to early August.

The Royals put together a fine performance against the home side at Pierce Memorial Stadium, but the Stingrays stung last, scoring two goals in the final 18 minutes to win 3-2. There was dejection — but no dissension — after the game. Gonzalo's post-game comments reflected the positive mood.

"Hey, it's not the end of the world," he said. "You guys played a great game, you had tough luck. You should be happy. We played a good game."

One of the better performers for the Royals was goalkeeper Andrew Scogna. His soccer career is laced with political intrigue and a journeyman's spirit. His freshman and sophomore seasons at George Mason University were distracted during a time of extreme personal challenge. His 20-year-old brother, Jared, and father, Paul, a U.S. diplomat stationed in Kuwait, were held hostage for several months in the U.S. embassy there after Iraq invaded Kuwait in 1990.

Andrew Scogna had a successful, but brief, stint in goal during the New England trip.

Scogna could have been a hostage as well, but instead of joining his brother and father in Kuwait, he chose to stay home and try out for George Mason's varsity team. Scogna had played soccer at Falls Church High School along with Royals teammate Alberto Ogando. He called Falls Church a "less than prestigious soccer high school." The head soccer coach was also a school football coach. "We pretty much coached ourselves," he said. "The coaching was poor and he really didn't help us with college."

Scogna made the team at George Mason but left following his sophomore year without playing in a game. He went to Dubai the following fall to live with his father but returned to the Washington area within the year. Scogna did not play soccer for two years, but stayed physically active by learning Kung Fu, ultimately reaching what he calls a "proficient" level.

Scogna seemed the most cerebral and philosophical of the Royals players, a reflection perhaps of his worldliness. He has lived in five countries. His talk is often graced with unimposing and enlightening perspective; his personality is as mellow as a pour of rich syrup.

During the earlier road trip to Reading—the first time Scogna dressed with the team—I shared a car ride with him and team manager John Ormassa. Scogna consumed much of the ride with introspective chatter about his past and ways of self-improvement, when not reading a book.

Scogna's return to soccer began as a keeper for the club Zorba, a high profile team in the NVSL's Premier Division. In the summer of 1996, the owner of Zorba made arrangements for Scogna to play with a top level club in Greece. Scogna had high hopes, but his trip was a farce.

"It was so shady it was ridiculous," he said. "Here I was in Athens and it's the summer and the team I was supposed to play with was not there because it was so hot. Apparently the club teams were playing somewhere in Switzerland, or something like that. I decided to stay because everybody told me the team was going to come back."

Scogna tried to make the best of a bad situation and trained hard on his own. "I ran every day," he said. " I came back really fit."

He stayed for half the summer and returned a wiser but more cynical man. He was asked if he was a little naive.

"You can say that," he said with a laugh. "I'm a little cynical when people talk to me about going places to play soccer."

The following spring and summer, in 1997, Scogna joined the Myrtle Beach SeaDawgs halfway through the season. He signed a contract with the SeaDawgs for $400 a month, but once he started playing the owners told him they could only afford to pay him $200 a month. He agreed to stay, and started a few games; the team did well, winning the Atlantic division with a 15-3 record and losing to Charlotte in the playoffs.

Scogna considered returning to Myrtle Beach for the 1998 season, but Gonzalo persuaded him instead to play for Iberia and then for the Royals.

Scogna thought during preseason that he had a good chance to win the starting position over Pascarella and Dia Kuykendall, a wispy keeper who played with a lot of heart. But Kuykendall, a regular keeper for Sheta's NVSL amateur team, Total Sports, lacked the professional experience of both Scogna and Pascarella.

Scogna's fortunes with the Royals nose-dived following scrimmages against a couple of Washington area colleges late in the preseason. He found out from Royals General Manager Sherif Shehata that he would not get paid when Shehata asked Scogna to sign a contract.

"I remember the next day; it was pouring rain," said Scogna. "I was in complete shock. They tried to make me out to be some greedy bastard. Hey, I'm trying to eat here. As soon as I started bitching, (goalkeeper) Jan (Da Weer) came in and Sherif (Shehata) starts calling him a true professional." Da Weer did not join the team until well into the preseason.

Three weeks after Scogna was told he would not get paid, Gonzalo announced after a practice what would become the final team roster. Scogna's name was not mentioned.

"We were all in a group and he read the names of the players he wanted to come back for the next practice," said Scogna.

Did Scogna ask Gonzalo why he was not picked?

"He didn't look me in the eye and I didn't want to talk to him about it," he said. "I thought it was hysterical because Silvino had been blowing sunshine up my ass for years. But I guess I saw it coming. I thought it was funny."

Gonzalo explained Scogna's dismissal as partially a matter of numbers. "I had four goalkeepers in training camp," he said. "I could only keep two on the roster. So I let Andrew and Dia (Kuykendall) go. The coach is always the enemy. Andrew, he's a nice guy. Mentally, he doesn't have it, but physically he has the tools to be good. He doesn't have the fire to be the best. That's what it takes to play the game. In the player's mind, he should think, 'there's nobody better than me.' "

Within one month—three games into the season—Shehata called Scogna to return to the Royals after Da Weer left the team.

"I like the people, but I just don't trust them," said Scogna of the Royals management. "You don't know where you stand. They use you whenever they can."

Still, Gonzalo gave Scogna's professional soccer pursuit a boost. In early September he arranged for the keeper to practice full-time with D.C. United, under the tutelage of famed goalkeeper coach Alan Kelly and along with MLS-proven keepers Mark Simpson, Scott Garlick and Tom Presthus.

"He will gain experience and will see how the professionals really work," said Gonzalo. "I told him 'I don't want you to make me look bad,' " he said, with a chuckle.

"From the beginning, I didn't feel like I didn't belong," said Scogna about training with United. "It's a little faster and the shots are a little harder than D3. It's not their fault, but I never got good goalkeeping training with the Royals. Matt (Badiee, the assistant coach who worked the keepers), did all he could. But I got more out of the first couple days with D.C. United than I got all season with the Royals."

Scogna hopes his training with D.C. United can get him a tryout at the MLS combine or an invitation to join the Maryland Mania, the new A-League team slated to begin during the 1999 season.

"I'm just starting to realize it's who you know," said Scogna. "I don't want to play D3. I have to move up to the A-League. How many years can you last playing like that in those kind of (D3) facilities? Your body won't hold up."

Scogna spoke with understandable resentment. His body would break down at the end of the trip to New England, ending his season before it had a real chance to begin.

After the 3-2 loss to Rhode Island, the team leaders—Rick Engelfried, Chris Jones and Steve Gill—shared a ride back to the team hotel in a van with Gonzalo. Since there was no locker room at the stadium, the players boarded the van quickly and still felt the emotion of a heartbreaking loss. Angst and frustration filled the 15-minute ride.

Jones sat in the front seat and instigated the passionate discussion.

"We came out and did not say 'We can win this thing!' he said. "We did not take it to them."

Engelfried echoed the message put forth by Jones. "The only time we lost the ball was when we got it in the 20-yard area in central midfield," he said."

Gill was more pointed in his assessment. "We don't have the personnel in midfield with the experience or skill level on this team," he said. "And we have to step up our game, be more vocal."

Gonzalo, who was driving the van, was quiet while he let his players express their feelings. By the time we pulled into the parking lot of the hotel, it was his turn to be heard. His brief message reflected his attitude that a soccer game was a war where everything was left on the field.

"You guys should get very angry and emotional during the game, not after the game," he said forcefully.

About an hour later, the team ate a relaxed dinner at an Italian restaurant near the hotel. The chatter was light and the conversation was comfortable. It is common for soccer players to toss back a few beverages of fermented barley and hops after a hard-fought game. But the Royals players instead drank milkshakes, iced tea, sodas and water.

Gonzalo's strict rule of no alcoholic beverages the night before a match would not be violated tonight, especially when the coach and team owner dined together about 20 feet away and the next game would start in a mere 15 hours.

I asked why no one was partaking in some post-game suds consumption. "You nuts?" said Engelfried, with a weary chuckle. "You think we want to get castrated?"

The Royals played the Cape Cod Crusaders the next day like a bunch of eunuchs. They showed little fight and some heart and were understandably fatigued. The Royals departed the hotel about 10 a.m. and arrived at Alan R. Carlson field, the Crusaders' home pitch, about an hour and a half before the 2 p.m. kickoff. The overcast sky and Cape Cod chill covered the field with a sense of impending doom. And a scant crowd of less than one hundred did nothing to lift the cloud of cold uncertainty that hovered over the Royals.

Gonzalo placed infrequently used Sean Lapier, a National Collegiate Athletic Association Division II All-America at Indiana University of Pennsylvania in 1990, up front in place of Trepal, who was nursing the aggravated hamstring injury. Jeff Todd, a strong and crafty midfielder, started his second consecutive game, replacing Adam Wilson at midfield. The Royals gave up a fluke goal in the sixth minute after a cross from the right side by the Crusaders fell easily and surprisingly inside the left post.

The Royals fell behind 2-0 at half time. Gonzalo knew his team was tired, so he was gentle with his half time oratory.

"I know your legs should be tired, but your minds should be fresh," he said. "Now we have to play. Get angry when you play, not after the game."

A testy Gill tried a more testosterone-laden approach. "This is the goddamn shittiest ass team we've ever played," he said.

An adulterous spouse couldn't get the Royals fired up in the second half. Their lethargy allowed a mediocre team to storm away with a 5-0 victory.

There was no screaming or other form of outward dissension by the players in their locker room after the game. They seemed too tired to muster the energy to complain. Players shuffled about methodically, saying and emoting very little. Sometimes, after a devastating loss like this one, against a team that is not five goals better than they were, players and coaches fall into a mild state of shock. These kinds of games are such an aberration that there's really not much anyone can say to put a proper perspective on what happened. During these times, sometimes it's best to let the players stew in their own juices, whether they are brews of indifference or obsessive introspection.

The most pressing concern seemed to be deciding where to eat and making sure Chris Jones and I got a ride to the airport on time. Jones had not been told about the rescheduled game the next day against New Hampshire until he boarded the plane in Baltimore at the start of the trip. With prior notice, he said he could have made arrangements to stay another day. But work beckoned, and he had to return home. I, too, needed to return home for work. Under trying circumstances, team management acted admirably to make sure we would make our flight on time.

The players were only mildly testy during a team meal about an hour later at a nearby restaurant. Chatter was comfortable, but it lacked the exuberance and light-heartedness evident during the post-game meal the night before. Two tough losses in two days can do that to a team.

Unfortunately, the Cape Cod Crusaders had chosen the same restaurant. They walked in en masse about five minutes after the Royals had ordered their meals. To their credit, their post-game victory mood was surprisingly restrained. Perhaps they didn't want to make it worse for their opponents.

The Crusaders wisely walked to the back portion of the restaurant, which was separated by a partition from the area where the Royals ate. It was hard not to notice, though, that the Crusaders, despite their graciousness, unknowingly managed to inflict some discomfort upon their opponents.

The Crusaders were drinking beer served in pitchers and poured into glistening, frosted mugs. Since the Royals had a game the next day, the no-

beer rule still applied. You could hear a mild groan or two as the wait-
ress walked repeatedly through the Royals' eating section carrying over-
flowing pitchers to the thirsty lads in the back. Could there have been
a more emphatic—however unintended—reminder of the spoils of winning?

The Royals miraculously played what Gonzalo called their best game
of the season some 30 hours later on artificial turf against the New
Hampshire Phantoms, a team which advanced to the D3 final four
later in the season. Despite their valiant effort, they lost 2-1.

The Royals departed New England physically battered and mentally weary. Their 2-6 record indicated a struggling team. The only consolation was that their last three losses were in U.S. Open Cup games
against teams that were not in their division. Take away the Cup games
and the Royals still stood dismally, but less tragically, at 1-3.

Injuries during the trip sidelined a few key players for the rest of
the season. In the New Hampshire game, Scogna severely sprained a
knee ligament after he leaped to tip the ball over the cross bar from a
corner kick. His knee twisted when he landed and his boots caught on
the unforgiving surface. Todd broke a foot in the New Hampshire game.
Devin Payton, one of the more dynamic players on the team, who scored
against Rhode Island, pulled a hip flexor in the game against Cape Cod
and missed the remainder of the season.

Further, the Royals' two most potent offensive weapons, Mahboub and Trepal, needed time to heal some bangs and strains after playing admirably throughout the trip despite obvious discomfort. Mahboub suffered a badly bruised ankle after he was chopped down in the
Rhode Island game and struggled against Cape Cod and New Hampshire. Trepal's strained hamstring was worse after the Rhode Island
game. He did not play against Cape Cod or New Hampshire and would
not return until the last couple games of the season.

Within one month, the Royals would become a transformed team.

FITTING IN

"It's much easier to get in shape than to stay in shape."
— Jumbo Elliott, former Villanova University track coach

The late Jumbo Elliott knew what he was talking about when it came to training elite runners. He coached for nearly a quarter century at Villanova for some of the top distance runners in the world, including Marty Liquori and Eamonn Coghlan. I ran against many of Elliott's great runners in the late 1970s and do not remember beating any of them. Elliott's track workouts were legendary for their intensity, lack of creativity and effectiveness. He often put his stable of distance runners through repeat quarter-mile intervals with an eighth-mile or quarter-mile jog in between. They commonly ran the intervals, up to 12 of them, in no slower than 60 seconds each. The tedium of those workouts can be mind-numbing. Staying focused and interested in such a workout was just as tough as enduring its physical discomfort.

Most elite athletes will tell you that it's easier getting into shape than staying in shape. Sure, the muscles will hurt a bit more when you begin pre-season training, but your mind is as eager as a Jack Russell terrier chasing a bleeding rabbit. Your muscles are relaxed and rested. It's hard, but, in a way, it's fun.

Strangely, I looked forward to the fitness workouts during practice with the Royals. I figured they couldn't be much worse than some of the interval training I endured with the University of Maryland track team. And since my soccer game favored speed and hustle rather than foot skill and trickery, the fitness sessions were comparatively easy for me.

The most punishing workout done by middle-distance runners while I ran for the University of Maryland was called a Murphy. It was set up as a ladder-type workout. The workout would start with two, 200-meter intervals done in about 30 seconds with 200-meter jogs in between. When in peak condition, we would then run 800 meters in just under 2 minutes, jog 800 meters, and then run the 200-meter intervals in about 25 seconds. Next came a 600-meter run in about 1 minute, 25 seconds, followed by a 600-meter jog and then the 200-meter intervals in about 25 seconds. Then came a 400-meter run in about 50 seconds, a 400-meter jog and the 200-meter intervals in about 25 seconds. Finally, we would try to cover 300 meters in about 36 seconds. A 300-meter jog and the 200-meter intervals followed. If coach felt a bit testy, we'd climb back up that ladder with times a little slower. What could be worse than that, I thought.

To avoid sitting in a wet parking lot, I sat on a cement car stop, slowly peeled off my waterlogged soccer boots and soggy socks and unlaced my wet ankle supports. My shorts were muddied and soaked. The clouded light of the fading day was passing with little inspiration. Coach Gonzalo must have sensed my misery.

"How do you feel, David," he asked cheerfully.

"Great, Silvino," I said with fake enthusiasm. "It feels good to run around in that shit."

I lied. Not about how good it felt to slog around on a puddle-marred and spongy field, but about how I felt. It didn't make sense for me to lie about that. I was not fighting for a spot on the team. There was no danger of being cut. I practiced at their pace to get a sense of what a professional soccer player endured during the course of a season. I felt I could practice with the team as long as I did not become a hazard to the other players.

It had been a long week of practice, the toughest I had experienced since I started training with the team on April 8. Practice began on that Friday, May 8 with the clouds spewing a steady torrent of rain. We played small-sided games of two-and-one-touch through the downpour that lasted about 20 minutes, and then continued for another hour or so. Toward the end of the game, my legs felt as heavy as a barrel of hay soaked in molasses. Nearly every touch went awry. I missed on every pass.

The practice week started for me on Monday with a light weight workout. The Royals had the day off after winning the day before. My amateur game on Sunday was canceled due to poor field conditions from heavy rain. So when Tuesday's practice arrived, I was sufficiently rested for a hard workout. And I was a bit excited when I showed up for practice and saw that Gayle Smith was milling about on the field.

This was not entirely because Smith—a former member of the U.S. Women's National Team—is an attractive and fit woman. Much of my excitement was from realizing that Smith's presence meant practice would include a grueling fitness session. Sound a little pathetic? Try to understand my frame of mind at the time. I felt extremely fit. It was time to test my fitness level.

Smith, a physical education teacher, works part-time as a personal fitness trainer and a youth soccer coach. Her top level of fitness and skills allows her to play effectively on top men's amateur teams in the Washington, D.C. area. She also plays for the Maryland Pride of the USISL W-League and is a member of Soccer Academy United of Clifton, Virginia, which won U.S. National Women's Amateur titles in 1996, 1997 and 1998. In early December, she was named to the U.S. Women's National "B" team.

Smith had trained the Royals, on occasion, since they began preseason training in January. Some players reminisced with lament about the intensity of Smith's workouts. More memories were forged by the end of Tuesday's practice.

Practice started with an easy 25-minute run through the rolling neighborhood of Avenel, an upscale community in suburban Maryland about 10 miles directly west of Washington, D.C.

After the run, we played a muck-marred, full-field game for 30 minutes or so. I wondered if playing on a field saturated with standing water brought any benefit. A muddy, wet field makes everything miserable. Balls bounce erratically and footing is greatly affected. But the Royals had little choice. The other option was to practice indoors at Sheta's soccer facility about an hour away. We had to endure the inconvenience outdoors.

For the fitness session—appropriately identified by Smith as "Death Warmed Over"—the team was split into groups of two. While one group ran, the other recovered. I volunteered for the first group for two reasons: 1) I wanted to get it over with as soon as possible; 2) it's unsettling psychologically to watch the group ahead of you suck wind, knowing that you would soon suffer similar discomfort.

Up to that point in the season—in early May— I had been given little chance to show Gonzalo how I could help his team. During the first month of practice, my goals were to test my body's resilience to practicing hard two or three times a week and then playing an amateur game on the weekend while the Royals played their games, and to be well accepted by my teammates. I tried to do whatever the coaches asked without complaining. I fetched balls behind the goal during shooting drills. I tried to pitch in however I could. Perhaps I kissed a little inconspicuous ass.

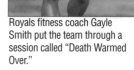

Royals fitness coach Gayle Smith put the team through a session called "Death Warmed Over."

Most importantly, I tried not to give the impression that I was there to take someone's spot on the roster. And up to that point, I don't think any player felt their team standing threatened by my efforts. The only real chance I had to show my skills was during games of keep-away, a common routine at the beginning of practice. The team would be split in two, sometimes up to 15 players to a side. All play was confined within about a half field. The games, varying from 10 minutes to 30 minutes long, were fast paced and forced you to react and think quickly. At the beginning, I was dreadful. I hadn't been subjected to such practice pressure since college. But by early May, my comfort level with the drill improved dramatically. I felt I was holding my own.

I viewed this first hard fitness session as a chance to exploit my assets. As I stood on the end line awaiting Smith's starting command, I felt anxiety and exhilaration. Anxiety for the pain I was about to endure, exhilaration for embarking on a true test of my fitness. They were feelings I experienced regularly before a hard track practice or competition in college.

The interval started at an end line. We ran to the near six-yard line and then back to the end line; to the near 18-yard line and back; to midfield and back; to the far 18-yard line and back; to the far six-yard line and back; to the far end line and back. The sense of pacing I learned from track training helped me considerably. Most teammates took the first half of the interval too hard. I tried to hang around the middle, hoping my endurance would benefit me in the end. It did. I finished among the top two in my group during each interval.

"The first set was supposed to make you think—okay, this will be tough but I should be able to do this," said Smith. "By the time you finished the second set, you should have wished it was over."

During the workout, Gonzalo stood at the far touchline to impart encouragement to players as they faced the long, final run to the other touchline. He praised my effort a couple of times.

"That's it, David," he said sternly and quietly. "Good job."

I could have done without one of the remarks he directed at the slower players.

"Come on, pick it up," he said. "He's almost twice your age." I was not insulted by the comment. Rather, I found it flattering. But I thought some of the players might hold it against me.

The first interval ultimately brought on a mild feeling of rigor mortis. By the end of the third, and last, interval, you understood the name of the workout. And we were only halfway through the fitness session.

The second set of intervals was shorter, but more intense. After a brief recovery period, we started at the end line and sprinted to the six-yard line and back three times. Five repetitions were done in that set. One group rested while the other group ran.

After about a 90-second recovery period, we started the final set, which involved sprinting from the end line to the 18-yard line and back three times.

That session was by far the toughest I experienced in training with the Royals. I apparently had missed some doozies during preseason.

Smith trained the team only a few times once the season began. But she worked with the team about a dozen times during preseason. Smith was good friends with Sheta, other members of management and some Royals players. She was one of two women who played regularly for Mo's Sports Shop, an amateur team in the NVSL's first division owned by Mo Sheta.

Smith watched the Royals' first two preseason practices to assess the fitness level of the players. For the third practice, she set up a fitness session that tested the players' commitment to fitness and promoted team unity.

"Since it was an early tryout, I tried to encourage the players to run hard and see what they were made of," said Smith. "You did not want a player on the team who was not willing to push and then have an attitude about it."

The drill Smith devised is usually done in a circle, but due to the large number of players—about 60—she gathered the players in a square. She broke up the players into groups of two, one led by Alberto Ogando and the other by Chris Jones. "I noticed during the first two days of practice that they could be leaders," she said.

The groups started jogging in a tight line. Upon Smith's prompt, the players performed various plyometric drills—short bursts of speed, jumps, hops and lateral runs. "I tried to simulate the changes of intensity that you go through in a game," she said.

The players then did a series of sprints where the last player in line sprinted to the front. As a further test, Smith had the player continue past the front of the line and sprint around the entire two groups before joining the front of the line. To mix things up, she had the sprinting player weave in and out of the players in front of him until he reached the front of the line.

If any player cut a corner as they ran in a square formation, the whole team had to do push-ups. "It happened only once, at least from what I could see," she said with a laugh.

Moments after our last interval during the session in May, some guys were slouched over, hands on their knees and gagging. Others walked with a wobble, heads tilted back heaving for air. A handful had already stopped after the first set of intervals.

Jones, one of the better runners on the team, was in my first group.

When the workout was over, I noticed, in a light-headed state, Jones walking slowly toward me. A high accumulation of lactic acid made his tightened muscles react with evident deliberation. I had walked toward the far touchline with my hands on my hips, trying to keep moving to more efficiently bring more air into my oxygen-debted muscles. As I turned back to the field, I spotted Jones flashing a cynical smile.

"I think we know who didn't play a game Sunday," he said.

Maybe his words included a subtle reminder to keep my success in perspective. But I considered it a sign that my efforts attracted attention. I had been noticed.

T he timing of the grueling fitness session threatened to help make me feel sluggish for a big game the next day. The first annual D.C. United Media Game beckoned at D.C. United Park, and I wanted to have fresh legs for the contest.

I attended dozens of practice sessions during D.C. United's first two seasons while I covered the team as a writer and its radio play-by-play announcer. Whenever I walked away from that complex, I wondered what it would be like to play on their immaculately-maintained practice pitch.

D.C. United managed to keep its main practice field in great condition. Their facility included an adjacent artificial turf field. If the natural turf field was unplayable, they merely had to move about 20 yards over and play on the astroturf.

It's hard to imagine a professional soccer facility in the U.S. better than United Park. Originally a training facility for the Washington Redskins before they moved in 1992, United Park sits on seven isolated acres in Herndon, Virginia. The 25,000-square-foot facility includes a strength training room, a rehabilitation room and a locker room that can comfortably accommodate three soccer teams. D.C. United is the only team in Major League Soccer to have both its business and practice facility in a single location.

By far the facility's most attractive feature is its main playing field. Surrounded by a fence high enough to keep intruders out and onlookers frustrated, the field is nearly full size. When you step on it, the ground soothes and embraces the bottom of the boot with cushioned comfort. Why romanticize a practice field? When you play soccer in the Washington, D.C. area, you face fields so bumpy, dirty and dry it is often wise to play in non-cleated shoes.

There was no need for me to bring my indoor boots at D.C. United Park. The incessant rains of the previous couple of weeks made United Park's main field a bit mushy. But it was firmer than the physiques of most of the journalists and media hacks who played in the game. Bulbous bellies and flabby muscles were more the norm.

The media members were split into print versus broadcast, the painters of prose versus the masseurs of the microphone. Because most of my soccer work has been in publishing, I was placed on the print team.

My plan was simple: run with pure abandon, since I was sure few others on the field could match my fitness. Within minutes of the opening whistle, it was clear our side was far superior. Will Kuhns, a writer for the *Washington Post*, controlled the match. He managed the central midfield with the flair and confidence of D.C. United's own Marco "El Diablo" Etcheverry.

I scored the first goal for our team. *Washington Times* writer John Haydon casually sent the ball into the box, where I was standing unmarked (no surprise there) about 12 yards out. I tapped it lightly into the goal.

Haydon scored twice in the first half to help us take a comfortable 6-1 lead, or something like that. I'd like to be more accurate about this but D.C. United's press staff did not provide an official game report. The lead was big. The teams were shuffled to even things up a bit in the second half, but the print scribes maintained their superiority.

I had a tough time maintaining my pace in the second half. I ran hard during the first half, covering the flank on both ends. But my legs tired by the middle of the second 30-minute period. I'll take any chance I can to offer an excuse, so here goes. The fitness workout with the Royals ended at about 8 p.m. the previous night. The media game began at noon the next day. I needed more than 16 hours—at least twice that—to recover well enough from a hard training session. It was not wise to play hard in a game so quickly—even against mostly unfit members of the media.

At the end of the game, I admit embarrassingly that I was beat a few times by others much less fit than I after I moved to outside back in the second half. I'd like to blame it on the referee, D.C. United Head Coach Bruce Arena, for missing some off-side calls. But that was not the case. Even if he missed some calls, I probably would not have said anything. He might not give me any more interviews.

I am exaggerating a bit here. But watching Arena at a press conference after a game—more so early in his career as D.C. United's coach—elicited uncomfortable feelings. A look of annoyance often covered his face. His answers were short and emotionless. A feeling of trepidation hovered in the interview room when Arena walked in, especially after a loss.

I often felt uncomfortable recording pregame interviews with Arena for the radio broadcasts because it seemed like it was such a bother to him. Many coaches love to chat it up in front of a microphone. It seemed Arena did not and would get up and walk away if I asked a wrong question. I've conducted lengthy, personal interviews with some high profile athletes—Pelé, John Harkes, Kareem Abdul Jabbar, Sugar Ray Leonard and Carl Lewis, to name a few. All potentially intimidating characters. None intimidated me more than Arena. But I learned that it was just his way of focusing before a game. And who can argue his successes?

Another side of Arena rarely seen is a compassionate, fun-loving sort who can yuck it up when around the right crowd. When Arena was Olympic head coach and D.C. United head coach in 1996, he staged a golf tournament between the Olympic players and D.C. United players. After the match, the players mingled with Arena, tossing back a few beers and swapping macho stories as if it were a fraternity party. Arena laughed and cavorted as much as the players. He has put up some of the younger D.C. United players—including 1998 MLS Rookie of the Year Ben Olsen—in his house.

I was not overly surprised when I saw Arena interacting comfortably with the media as the center referee for the match. This was his element—on a playing field, calling the shots. He laughed a bit and threw out a few off-handed comments.

Toward the end of the second half, Arena was having a better time than I was. The blood in my legs developed an annoying leaden quality and they felt ineffective. I spent the last 10 minutes or so staying back lazily on defense, helping ensure our team's lop-sided victory.

As I sat in my locker in D.C. United's dressing room after the game, a euphoric sense of accomplishment enveloped me. Never before had I so reclined in a professional locker room. Had John Riggins or Harkes used the locker in which I sat? Had Joe Gibbs or Arena walked down the rows of these same gated lockers, imparting some inspiring or encouraging words to his players? I lingered in that surreal environment for about 10 minutes, not saying much to anyone, just sitting in my metal locker encased by legendary athletic spirits. It was as close as I'd get to feeling like a top level professional soccer player. I walked out of that locker room with tangible mementos as well—a new D.C. United hat and T-shirt.

The day was capped off nicely with a free outdoor buffet luncheon with some of D.C. United's players and coaches. The Man of the Match award was announced and aptly awarded to Haydon for his four-goal effort.

I came away that day with a personal prize. I had endured two hard sessions in less than 24 hours without getting hurt. By the end of Wednesday, though, severe fatigue set in. I napped twice the next day. All I could muster for a workout on Thursday was a set of push-ups and sit-ups along with light stretching.

Gonzalo kept the Royals practice light on Friday since they had a game scheduled for Sunday. After a 30-minute game, we ran about a dozen hard sprints up a steep, short hill. Each sprint began with a tumble to simulate quick recovery after a fall. They were fun, but I felt dizzy every time I raised up from the roll to start the sprint.

Just one week before, I noted in my diary that practicing with the Royals had become a welcome reprieve from work and the monotony of working out on my own. I was exhilarated that my body was enduring two successive days of hard practice and, on average, three days of practices per week. The last time I practiced so hard was in college more than 20 years ago.

The incessant hard running, turning and twisting can easily break down 40-year-old bones and muscles to the point of injury. I was pleasantly surprised that I felt no regular or impairing pain.

Everything felt drastically different one week later. As I struggled in the parking lot to pull on a dry, clean pair of socks to wear home after Friday's practice, I realized for the first time that practice was becoming a nuisance. I had passed up a social gathering that began about the same time I had arrived for practice. My social life was beginning to suffer. Fatigue consumed my body and my mind. It was tough to maintain my work schedule. I started to appreciate what my teammates were going through: the commitment to practicing regularly and staying fit on their own while working full-time; sacrificing socializing with friends to make weekend trips to games.

I mostly enjoyed the training and practicing. But I needed a break. And I still had three months to go.

8

MID-SEASON EBB AND FLOW

A t about 9:30 a.m. on Tuesday morning, May 19, following the the weekend in New England where the Royals lost three games, Silvino Gonzalo is fighting lingering fatigue. He had been home barely an hour. The flight from Greene Airport in Providence, Rhode Island departed just before 7 a.m. and had arrived in Baltimore a little after 8 a.m. With only a few hours sleep the night before, Gonzalo was experiencing an unpleasant soccer hang over.

As he talked on the phone, reminiscing candidly—and perhaps cathartically—about the previous few days and the season thus far, the strain in his voice reflected his weary state of mind and the struggles of his team.

After losing 5-0 to Cape Cod on May 17, Gonzalo had gathered his troops at the team hotel for an unpleasant meeting.

"I told them that I was not going to stay around," he said. "I thanked them for playing but that I must go. I was angry. It was embarrassing for me. I hate to do a job where I'm not doing what I know I can do, and disappoint the owners of the organization, my fans and friends. This is not good for my ego and my well-being. I know these players can do it and they are good. That's very disappointing to me. I told Mo (Sheta) coming back from the trip that I don't mind if you tell Silvino that you've found somebody else (to coach the team)."

During half time of the New Hampshire loss, Gonzalo again blew a fuse. "The first half was poor," he said. "They were doing everything wrong. I got very angry, and then I forgot that we played two previous games. But then I don't care if we play five games in one week. I want it to be played my way."

Some six weeks into the regular season, Gonzalo was for the first time in his coaching career involved with a losing team. It had been a learning experience for him as much as for his players.

"We call ourselves professionals but we are not professionals," he said. "You have to compensate the players with something for them to be motivated and feel good about it. I approach this a little like an amateur team. Sometimes the players come to practice and it's not there. Sometimes it's tough asking these kids to do things. I can see sometimes when they come to training that they come from the office, listening to screaming, and then they have to hear it from me. We have to rush to practice; sometimes we don't eat. Their concentration is sometimes not there. Sometimes they are just out there."

Despite his concerns, Gonzalo had not lost faith in his team.

"I have a great feeling about what I'm am trying to do," he said. "I want a team that will get angry if we lose. That's what I demand of my players. I am very optimistic. We will make the playoffs this season. This may sound stupid, but by the end of the season, we will be a very respectable team."

The Royals returned to respectability the following weekend with what Gonzalo called "a very good game" against "opposition that was not very good." The result was a 3-2 win over the winless Eastern Shore Sharks, also a first-year team.

The game started precariously for the Royals. The Sharks scored first in the 26th minute. But the Royals came back two minutes later with their first goal, scored by Jeff Standish, who had played sparingly for the Royals up to that point.

It would be the only goal scored all season by Standish, a 28-year-old central midfielder and defender from White Plains, New York who lists "beer drinking" as a hobby. Standish, a four-year starter and captain at Colgate University, was a two-year veteran of D3 play before he joined the Royals. He played for the Philadelphia Freedom outdoor team and the Baltimore Bays indoor and outdoor teams, both now defunct.

Jan Da Weer, who also played for the Bays, convinced Standish to try out for the Royals. They missed the beginning of preseason training while still playing for the Bays indoor team; they joined the Royals about two weeks before the home opener.

"Playing for the Bays and the Freedom was more professional," said Standish. "A lot of that may be due to the fact the Royals were a first-year team."

Like some other Royals players, Standish thought at the beginning of the season that he would get paid. "There was an article in the *Washington Post* stating that the majority of players would get some kind of compensation," he said.

The *Post* article appeared on April 10, the day of the Royals' home and season opener. It stated that top players could earn $5,000 for the season and that most would earn between $75 and $200 per game. Midway through the season, no player had been paid and by that time the players had accepted the fact that no money would be forthcoming.

Standish, an analyst for the International Center for Technology in Rockville, Maryland, was not playing soccer to make lots of money. He was used to making a mere pittance playing in D3. The Bays paid him $50 a game. With the Freedom, he earned nothing if the team did not win. The payments for a win were $25 for sitting the bench, $50 for playing and $75 for starting.

Standish, one of the most professionally experienced players on the team, started less than half the games for the Royals. Once he sensed a lack of commitment from Gonzalo, he adjusted his approach to the team.

"It became clear to me pretty early that Silvino was not making a commitment to me," he said. "Even though Silvino and I got along off the field, on the field our styles clashed. I made a decision early in the season that other things in my life were going to take precedence. I didn't feel like I got a fair shake from Silvino to prove myself on the field. He had no explanation for why I was not starting."

Gonzalo felt Standish was not a team player. "He thinks he probably is the best player on the team, but I don't think so," he said. "I wanted him to be a team player and he's not. He can be good. But he's not as good as he thinks he is. That's the problem sometimes with American players. They come from an American system and they think that's the only system. I have to be honest—his attitude sometimes when I talked to him sounded sarcastic."

Standish felt he faced a disadvantage for not having played before for Gonzalo. "I felt slighted because I had not played for Silvino before that," he said. "A lot of it might have been a language thing. His communicating was hard to understand. It was all part of the frustration."

One Royals player more comfortable with Gonzalo and the team's situation is Alberto Ogando, who provided the Royals with a lift just before half time of the Sharks game with a score in the 44th minute.

Midfielder Alberto Ogando was one of the more reliable players for the Royals.

Ogando also tallied seven minutes into the second half, putting the Royals up 3-1. He proved to be one of the more reliable players for the Royals. A native of Wilmington, Delaware with Spanish heritage, Ogando plays the game with a strong Latin passion.

Positioned mostly on the left flank, Ogando displayed consistent ruggedness and a ferocious flair. His undaunted spirit often infused energy into the Royals' attack. One of the more fit players on the team, Ogando worked hard on conditioning in practice, often finishing near the front in various sprint workouts.

Ogando, 27, attained *Washington Post* All-Metropolitan and All-Region honors at Falls Church High School, where he was a teammate of Royals goalie Andrew Scogna. Ogando later played for the U-19 VISTA Force, which reached the final four at the national youth championships in 1989, and was a Junior College All-American at Montgomery Junior College in Maryland. Ogando played for Sheta on his amateur team, Total Fitness.

Ogando aspires to a higher level of professional soccer than D3 and Gonzalo surely would do everything he could to help secure future success for him. Gonzalo and Ogando share a common Spanish bond. Gonzalo was born and raised there; Ogando's parents lived much of their lives there.

"My dad always wanted me to play," said Ogando.

Ogando and Gonzalo often communicated in a dialect that was part Portuguese and part Spanish, both in practice and in games, offering a sense of intrigue to either setting. I often wondered what were they talking about.

There was little question about Ogando's scoring prowess. He finished the season second on the team in goals scored with six. And when he wanted to play, he played relentlessly with the hardened heart of a true outside midfielder. But at times he would disappear from a game's flow, flashing periods of apparent disinterest.

Ｗith Scogna injured and John Pascarella still on the West Coast at a wedding, Gonzalo asked D.C. United for some help in goal against the Sharks. This time, instead of Mark Simpson they sent down Tom Presthus, who was at that time a reserve keeper. Presthus would eventually start 12 games for D.C. United—all at the end of the season—and lead them to a third consecutive MLS Cup appearance. It was the only game Presthus would play for the Royals, and although the team gave up two goals, he was relatively untested and faced only a few shots.

Against the Sharks, the Royals had applied heavy midfield pressure—something Gonzalo had preached emphatically and rather unsuccessfully—and had attacked aggressively and built well from the back. They were aided by two new elements in central midfield. Brad Agoos, the brother of D.C. United and National Team star Jeff Agoos, was also on loan from D.C. United. Brad Agoos had been practicing with D.C. United when United assistant coach Dave Sarachan called Gonzalo to see if Agoos could get some playing time.

The other pleasant surprise was the reinvigorated play of Adam Wilson. "Adam was a completely different player," said Gonzalo. "I told him to play the way I want or he sits the bench. He played tremendously and I gained confidence with him again. I had completely lost it. Adam was a completely different player. He played very good defense."

It is no surprise that Gonzalo talked about Wilson with much passion. No player suffered the wrath of Gonzalo's emotional tirades more than Wilson. During many heated half time gatherings, mostly in the midst of a poor Royals effort, Gonzalo singled out Wilson for bad play or for not listening to him.

Midfielder Adam Wilson suffered the constant wrath of coach Silvino Gonzalo.

At half time of the Rhode Island game during the trip to New England, Gonzalo berated Wilson for asking a referee who a Royals substitute was replacing in the first half.

"Adam," he said in full rage, "this is the last time you ask a referee who a player is going in for. That's my fucking decision. Don't worry about who's going in. Worry about the game."

It seemed that Wilson received some kind of verbal attack nearly every time Gonzalo was mad at the team. I made light of that quandary as I walked to a half time session during a home match against the South Carolina Shamrocks in late June. The Royals had played a less than impressive first half.

Anticipating an irate Gonzalo, I said to Wilson, who did not dress for the match and was walking with me, "At least he can't pick on you."

"Yeah, you got that right," he said with relief.

Throughout the season, Wilson tolerated the criticism well. He mostly absorbed Gonzalo's urgings by saying nothing. A few times, though, he did try to defend himself. But he soon learned that that tactic only made the situation worse.

Wilson, 23, was an All-District and All-Region selection while playing at Stonewall Jackson High School in Manassas, Virginia. He was also picked for U-17 and U-18 state and regional ODP teams.

Wilson was one of the stronger free spirits on the team. He sported yellow hair, bracelets and an earring or two, even while practicing. Wilson displayed little interest in material worth. He lived with his parents and did not work much of the season.

"I don't have a car," he said with mild concern toward the end of the season. "Mine blew up. I need to find a job and go back to school."

Gordon Bradley, the famed former coach of Pelé and Franz Beckenbauer with the New York Cosmos of the North American Soccer League, coached Wilson at George Mason University.

"He's a different kettle of fish," he said of Wilson.

Wilson became a solid force at midfield for Mason his last two years there before his eligibility expired in 1997. Five classes short of a degree in health, fitness and recreation resources, Wilson started plotting a path for a career in professional soccer.

After leaving Mason, Wilson started playing locally with Total Fitness in the NVSL. By the following winter he had completed successful try-outs with the Staten Island Vipers and the Hampton Roads Mariners, both in the A-League. The Vipers offered him $1,500 a month and a bonus of $250 per start. The Mariners offered Wilson an apartment and $1,000 a month.

Wilson was set to move to New York to play with the Vipers, but he turned it down to play for the Royals. He had played well for Gonzalo on the 1997 Virginia State team at the Donnelly Cup, where they finished second. Wilson had four goals and four assists in three games at the tournament.

Wilson said he understood from his initial discussions with Sheta that he would get paid to play for the Royals. But shortly before the season began, he found out there would be no money.

"That was a reason I had a problem with a decision about playing for the Royals or taking an A-League offer," he said. "I thought I was going to get paid."

Why did he decide to stay with the Royals?

"Silvino knows a lot of players and I figured he had some connections with other teams," he said. "It was close to home and I thought we'd be doing better than we are doing."

Wilson, sitting on a small set of bleachers in mid-July, reflected on his soccer situation during a practice as the team worked out on the field. He is one of the few Royals players who would like to play in Major League Soccer, ultimately with D.C. United.

"I'm trying to get in with D.C. United," he said. "If they asked me to practice for one year with no money, I'd do it."

Next year he said he hopes to jump up to the A-League, possibly with the Maryland Mania, which will debut in Baltimore during the 1999 season.

But first, Wilson had to endure a tough first campaign with the Royals. A starter at the beginning of the season, Wilson had lost Gonzalo's confidence with a month remaining in the season and the Royals battling for a playoff spot.

Wilson was sitting on the bleachers because Gonzalo removed him from a practice game against a local amateur team. Typically, he was perplexed about why he was not playing.

"As always, I did nothing," he said. "I think he thought I fouled somebody, but I didn't."

Wilson seemed to be at a crossroads in his pursuit of an MLS career. Had he asked Gonzalo why he's not playing?

"Yeah, he says he wants me to do certain things, to mark tighter," he said. "In a practice game my mark touches the ball twice and I still get yelled at."

Would he quit?

"I've thought about it. But I've never quit anything in my life. And I'm all right with it now. If he's gonna play his game, I can't do anything about it."

Why does he think he's not starting? "Do you want me to tell you what I really feel? This team is made up of two teams," he said. "Mo's team (Total Fitness) and Silvino's team (Iberia). You can do no wrong if you're one of (Silvino's) boys. If not, you get blamed for everything."

Gonzalo countered Wilson's claim of favoritism, but also said he might have been a bit too hard on him.

"I respect that comment, but he is wrong," said Gonzalo after the season. "I suspended Steve Gill from the team, and he is one of my older players (from Iberia). I had a lot of hope for (Wilson) to do good because I think he is a good player. He has the skills to be a creative player, but he lacks the concentration and mentality to be a creative midfielder. I probably was too hard on him, but I was trying to see if I could awaken his mind."

Bradley feels Wilson has tremendous skill and commitment to soccer. He saw Wilson improve dramatically during his last two years at George Mason to a level that he showed against the Sharks.

"A lot of players are not too comfortable on the ball," said Bradley. "Adam would like the ball for 90 minutes. He'll take the ball off you anytime. Adam loves the game. He'll play 24 hours a day. His problem is he would do his own thing all the time and would do things that would promote his game and improve his game. He was predictable. There's nothing wrong with that as long as you execute well. But you can't be a better player if at times you are a bit predictable."

Where does Wilson feel he needs to improve?

"I need more consistency," he said.

Wilson was probably the most fit athlete on the team, due to a combination of genetics and determination. He sports a lean, ectomorphic musculature and 4.5 percent body fat. He often trained two or three times a day, performing plyometrics and finishing drills with his brother, Curtis, a youth coach in the area who trained early in the season with the Royals. He also trained with Gayle Smith, the Royals' fitness coach.

By the end of the season, Wilson spent more time on the bench than on the field. And he endured more verbal assaults by Gonzalo.

"What I see in Silvino is he knows who he can shout at," said Bradley, who has watched Gonzalo coach throughout the 1980s and 1990s. "Adam has the personality that he won't complain."

W ilson continued his steady play after the win over the Sharks during a two-game road trip against the South Carolina Shamrocks and the Charlotte Eagles. While Wilson returned to a prominent role with the Royals, his childhood pal Scott Poirier had become a significant non-factor. Poirier had not played a game in about a month, appearing last against the Reading Rage on May 1. When Gonzalo announced the 15-man roster at the end of practice the day before the trip to the Carolinas, Poirier was surprised Gonzalo did not call his name.

After the team dispersed, Poirier quickly approached Gonzalo for an explanation. They talked quietly for about half a minute and then Poirier walked away slowly towards his car in pensive loneliness, looking straight down at the ground.

Minutes later, Gonzalo explained why Poirier was not picked for the trip. "He has great potential, but he has not shown it the last couple of weeks," said Gonzalo. "He has to be more aggressive. If he does what I tell him, he will be one of the best players on the team."

However, Poirier did eventually make the trip. Sweeper Steve Gill was called home after the South Carolina game on Friday night when his wife became ill. Poirier replaced Gill on the roster and played the last 15 minutes of the Charlotte game on Saturday night.

There was other player shuffling as well. Gonzalo decided to take just 13 players for the South Carolina game, but Brad Agoos missed the ride with the team Friday morning. He joined the team the next day for the game against Charlotte. That forced the Royals to start the South Carolina game with one substitute — goalkeeper Dia Kuykendall. And the rarely-used keeper was almost called off the bench as a field player after Justin Kerns strained a hamstring five minutes into the match.

Typically, Kerns toughed it out and finished the game.

"I knew (the hamstring) was done as soon as it happened," he said. "But I had to keep playing because we had just one player on the bench and it was a goalkeeper. It started bleeding badly after the game."

The injury forced Kerns to miss four games throughout the rest of the season. But when he played, he was a steady stopper for the Royals.

Kerns is a rugged man marker who plays with as much heart as anyone on the Royals' roster. His journey toward becoming a regular contributor to the Royals contrasts dramatically from his teammates. As a result, his ambitions and expectations with the team are less lofty than his Royals comrades.

The soft-spoken Kerns is the only frequent starter to not play on the varsity teams at his high school or college. Kerns played tennis and ran cross-country at Clarke County High School in Winchester, Virginia, but didn't play soccer because the school did not have a boys soccer team. He did not play at Virginia Tech because the coach discouraged walk-ons trying out for the team.

Defender Justin Kerns, listening to assistant coach Matt Badiee, never played high school or college soccer.

Kerns, 30, followed a path similar to most of his teammates, though, by starting to play the game at an early age—six years old. While living in Alexandria, Virginia, he played in the Herndon Youth League until he was 11. After he moved with his family to Berryville to escape the rapidly congesting Washington, D.C. area, Kerns played for a Loudoun County youth club for a year and half before tearing ligaments in a knee. The injury forced him out of the game for about one year. When he returned, Kerns played in adult recreational leagues throughout high school since there were no quality youth clubs to play for in the Winchester or Leesburg, Virginia areas.

Kerns played on recreational teams throughout college. After graduating, Kerns started playing in the NVSL with friends from college. Soon after, his aspirations for soccer became more intense. A friend from Costa Rica convinced Kerns to join him in trying out for a lower-division professional club in Costa Rica. "I felt confident that my playing level was all right and my friend thought I could play there," he said.

But the Costa Rican experiment lasted only three weeks. "All they could offer was room and board and I just wasn't ready to leave the U.S.," he said. "I never got a legitimate offer."

In 1992, Kerns met Royals owner Mo Sheta while playing against Sheta's teams in the NVSL. Later, while playing an indoor game at Sheta's Total Sports Pavilion, Kerns was asked by Sheta to join his outdoor team,

Total Sports.

Kerns played several years for Total Sports and Mo's Sports Shop. In the fall of 1997, Kerns, a systems analyst for SRA, was transferred to New Orleans. But he returned to the Washington area after Sheta called him the following February to try out for the Royals.

After a week of tryouts, Kerns told Gonzalo that he needed to know if the Royals would sign him so he could ask for a permanent job transfer back to Washington. Kerns signed a three-year contract with the Royals. He had no problem with not getting paid.

"It was an opportunity that I would never get again," said Kerns, who lives in Centreville. "I'm 30 years old. I wanted to prove that I could play at that level."

One player who had proven he can play at almost any level is Mark Simpson, the former MLS Cup winning keeper with D.C. United. Against South Carolina, the game after the Royals' 3-2 win over the Eastern Shore Sharks, Simpson made his second start for the Royals. It marked the third time in 10 games that Gonzalo started a D.C. United keeper in goal.

Gonzalo was clearly unhappy with his goalkeeper situation. Scogna was out with injury and Pascarella, although back from his 10-day West Coast trip, had not played steadily enough to become the regular starting keeper. Gonzalo called Kuykendall's performance against New Hampshire "very good" after replacing the injured Scogna, but he had not yet earned the coach's full confidence. And Simpson, pushed back to reserve keeper on D.C. United's roster, was looking for some playing time.

Gonzalo explained the reason for using Simpson in goal. "I don't want to not appreciate the goalkeepers we have, but if I think that they will help the team, I will use whoever is best," he said. "Simpson is at a different level than our other keepers. I think he is probably one of the best keepers in the country. When you have a keeper of that level, you can take more chances."

Against the Shamrocks, Ogando took some pressure off the defense when he scored the game's first goal midway through the first half. It was his third goal in two games and his third consecutive tally for the Royals. But the Shamrocks scored two quick goals to lead 2-1 at half time. Rachid

Mahboub worked brilliantly around two Shamrock defenders and scored about midway through the second half to send the game into overtime.

Similar to its first overtime effort of the year—the season opening 3-2 win—the Royals waited until the last couple of minutes to steal a win. Tim Prisco's shot with 1:35 remaining in the 15-minute overtime period rebounded to Tony Trepal, who pushed the ball in the net for the clincher.

Prisco's assist was the first point he scored for the Royals all season and symbolized the increasing role he would develop with the team. After recovering from an ankle injury, Prisco joined the Royals in mid-May. It was a dramatic way to make his Royals debut two weeks later.

Prisco was moved to his more natural position at inside midfield the next day against the Charlotte Eagles. The Royals played one of their better games of the season despite the overtime battle that ended less than 20 hours before kickoff against Charlotte. The Royals lost 2-0 to Charlotte, but their third road trip of the season was dramatically more successful than their horrid adventure in New England. They lost one of two games, but played two good games in a row for the first time all season.

Halfway through their first season, with a 4-7 record (2-2 in the conference) and still in the hunt for a playoff berth, were the Royals finally showing signs of cohesiveness and developing a sense of purpose?

NO MAGIC, MUCH WRATH

The Delaware Wizards reflect a flourishing franchise that the Northern Virginia Royals aspire to emulate and the USISL proudly calls one of its own. The Wizards are a sixth-year franchise with strong corporate support, a supportive and enthusiastic local soccer community and a solid marketing and promotional approach. They're remarkably successful on the field as well. In 1998, they won the Atlantic Division and made it to the national quarterfinals.

The Wizards and the Delaware Genies, its sister team in the USISL's W-League, have similar owners under different names to protect the amateur status of the Genies. Firststate Soccer, which owns the Wizards, includes a full set of corporate officers—president, vice-president, secretary and treasurer—and a support staff that includes directors of finance, public relations, marketing and ticket sales; three trainers; a team physician; a team orthopedic surgeon; a team chiropractor and a team podiatrist. The Wizards did not lose money during a couple of its seasons, something they considered successful.

The team plays its home games on the main athletic field at McKean

High School, an old soccer-friendly facility just south of Wilmington. No running track circles the field, like at many other D3 game fields. The pitch was adequately manicured and a good size (110 yards long, 68 yards wide). The wooden bleachers can comfortably accommodate 3,000 spectators. A large, grassy recreating area with picnic benches sits invitingly behind and to the side of one of the goals. It's a prime and safe place for toddlers to frolic and expend energy while the parents and older kids watch the game with little interruption.

The Wizards' team yearbook, sold for one dollar, is produced in full magazine, four-color format and boasts advertising on more than half its 44 pages. One full-page ad listed more than one dozen weeks for the team's summer camps, which USISL team owners know is a prime source of ancillary revenue and a great opportunity for team members to make extra money.

The Genies listed four high profile members of the U.S. Women's National Team—midfielders Kristin Lilly and Tisha Venturini, forward Debbie Keller and goalkeeper Briana Scurry—on its roster. Just two—Lilly and Keller—played in the Genies game that preceded the Royals match against the Wizards. That did not bode well for the Royals, however, because the presence of the Women's National Team players affected attendance, in the Wizards favor.

The stadium was half full when the Royals took the field on a comfortably warm evening on June 6 to face the Wizards for the second and final time of the season. The Royals were trying to avenge a 1-0 loss to the Wizards in late April. Further, the Royals were tied with the Wizards in third place in the eight-team Atlantic Division midway through the 1998 campaign. But the Royals stood just three points ahead of the seventh place team. The top six teams advanced to the playoffs.

The game marked the return of John Pascarella in goal and the emergence of frisky midfielder Tim Prisco and pesky outside defender Adam Vigon.

Prisco, 24, moves along the pitch like a crafty cat. At 5 feet, 9 inches tall and 145 pounds, Prisco does not win balls or move down the field with imposing strength. Instead, he relies on tremendous quickness and fleet-footedness. Prisco's introverted demeanor contrasts greatly with his dynamism on the pitch, where his method is the prolonged run or the surprise attack.

A native of Dale City, Virginia, Prisco won five Virginia Youth Soccer Association State Cup titles with the Prince William Sparklers and the Springfield Cobras. He was a *Washington Post* All-Met selection at Garfield High School and a full-time starter for William & Mary University by the time he left the school after his sophomore season. Although a starter, Prisco's final two years of collegiate play at the University of Virginia were marred by ankle injuries that sidelined him half of each season.

Prisco, who yearns to play in Major League Soccer, joined the Royals after he called team owner Mo Sheta in mid May 1998. Prisco had played for Sheta's team, Total Fitness, off and on for three years before taking a year off following ankle surgery in June 1997. When he called Sheta, Prisco had not played competitive soccer since the surgery.

Midfielder Tim Prisco brought quickness and flair to the Royals midfield.

He would not feel game-fit until the end of the season, but Prisco injected much-needed quickness and pace at midfield for the Royals. He made a profound third appearance as a Royal in the away contest against the Wizards by scoring the team's only goal.

Vigon, 28, made his debut for the Royals the weekend before the Wizards match against the South Carolina Shamrocks. A chipper chap from Manchester, England, Vigon boasts quick feet, sure skill and good speed. He once dreamed of soccer stardom in his homeland and consequently endured the gritty world of soccer journeymen.

Vigon played for top youth teams with the Oldham Athletic Club near Manchester while attending school. But after he turned 16, he became a soccer apprentice and spent most of this time playing in an environment that promoted little intellectual stimulation.

"I spent a hard two-and-a-half years playing tough soccer full time, talking about beer and sex and taking a piss out of (picking on) each other," he said with some fond relish and a laugh after a practice in early June. "We would train in the morning and most of the lads would play the horses in the afternoon. They were not well-educated."

As an apprentice, Vigon was responsible for cleaning the lockers and maintaining the equipment of some veteran players.

"I shined a lot of boots for some of the boys," he said with humble pride.

Vigon reached the paid professional level for a couple of months. He played in the second division with Stockport, making about $150 per week.

Vigon abandoned soccer full-time at age 20 after being released from Stockport. He then returned to school full time.

"It felt good to use my brain again," he said.

Vigon came to the United States to study political science and play soccer for Davis & Elkins College, an NCAA Division II school in West Virginia. He played there for two years before transferring to the University of Charleston, another Division II school in West Virginia. During his first year at Charleston as a junior, the school finished 17-2-1 and was ranked as high as third in the country.

Speedy defender Adam Vigon played a bit with a second division British club.

Before the 1998 season, Vigon had planned to try out for the South Carolina Shamrocks. But he opted to stay in the Washington area and live with his fiancée. Vigon learned of the Royals via the Internet and joined the team the first week of May.

While Vigon had established himself as a starting back for the Royals, Pascarella was still a concern. Due to personal commitments, serving a red card suspension and the availability of D.C. United keepers Mark Simpson and Tom Presthus, Pascarella had not played a game in more than a month. And he missed nearly two weeks of team training while on holiday in California in May. The Wizards game would mark the first time he would be in goal supporting defender Chris Jones since their locker room tussle in Reading. As it turned out, Jones and Pascarella showed no signs of animosity. In fact, they got along fine. Just moments before the start of the second half, the two shared a laugh as they walked back onto the pitch.

Pascarella's play did not hamper the Royals. Instead, they again lost the battle in the middle of the field with inadequate defensive pressure. The Wizards' superior speed in the middle of the offensive attack exposed the lack of pace in the Royals central defense, with Steve Gill at sweeper and Rick Engelfried playing stopper. The Wizards led the Royals 2-0 at half time.

Prisco, starting at central midfield for the first time, pulled the Royals to within one early in the second half when he kicked in a loose ball from about 10 yards in front of the goal. The Royals applied relentless pressure over the next 10 minutes and narrowly missed a chance to tie the game when Matt Ferry's hard header was barely tipped over the cross bar.

But then momentum swung as the Royals ran out of gas. With about 18 minutes remaining, Gonzalo lost whatever patience that lingered for his overmatched central defense. Moments after a quick counter through that part of the field led to a goal, putting the Wizards up 3-1, he turned, red-faced and arms waving, and walked toward General Manager Sherif Shehata, standing next to Mo Sheta on a hill behind the team bench.

"I don't care what the rules are, sign that guy from A.U.," he screamed, referring to Steve Franzke. Gonzalo had been courting Franzke, a swift and solid central defender who helped lead American University to the NCAA Tournament quarterfinals in 1997, for more than a month.

With four minutes left, Steve Gill's frustration led to yet another red card for the Royals for a dangerous tackle. The Wizards had already scored their final goal on another counter down the middle.

The Royals played gallantly until the last 20 minutes. But the disappointing end was all that remained in owner Mo Sheta's mind as he walked off the field following the game.

"Very embarrassing," he said to no one in particular, his head shaking in bewilderment.

After the loss to Delaware, the Royals, with a 4-8 record, faced a critical part of its schedule. Of its next four games — all at home — the Royals were to face three of the four teams that were tied with them or who trailed them in the standings. South Carolina was one point behind and Wilmington two points behind. The first opponent was the Roanoke Wrath. The Wrath had three wins and four losses and were tied with the Royals in fourth place with nine points.

Although a first-year team in D3, the Wrath was a veteran USISL club. They played the 1995 and 1996 seasons as the Roanoke Riverdawgs in the USISL's Premier Development Soccer League, the level below D3 that features all amateur teams. New owners stepped in in 1997 and changed the name to the Roanoke Wrath. In 1997 the Wrath played 13 exhibition games as an amateur club.

For the 1998 season, the Wrath managed a coup when they signed Mike Fisher, a 1996 collegiate Player of the Year from the University of Virginia. Fisher was picked second overall in the 1997 Major League Soccer college draft but he chose medical school over an MLS career. Fisher played four games with the Wrath in 1998 and scored one goal. He spent most of the summer of 1998 with his parents in New Jersey.

The most telling statistic about the Wrath's potential was that their goals for (12) was nearly double their goals allowed (7). They were struggling, but not as badly as the Royals, whose goals-for-to-goals-allowed ratio stood at 11-21.

As I entered the field about 30 minutes before game time, I spotted Mark Simpson standing near the Royals bench, preparing to warm up. He greeted me with a lighthearted comment.

"What are you doing wasting your time coming out here on a Saturday night?" he said half jokingly as we shook hands. It was clear that his lack of playing time with D.C. United coupled with perhaps too many appearances with the Royals in D3 made Simpson a bit testy. Surely, the 100 or so spectators in the bleachers failed to completely stimulate Simpson's competitive juices.

We talked about his situation with D.C. United. "I'm just waiting for

(D.C. United Head Coach) Bruce (Arena) to give me a chance," he said. Perhaps that frustration fueled Simpson to one of his more passionate performances with the Royals.

However, the game nearly did not count. An afternoon thunderstorm caused a power outage in the area near the field. As a result, the scoreboard and field lights were inoperable when the game began. The game proceeded on time, but if conditions were unplayable before the first half was completed, it could have been rescheduled. A game counts if a first half is completed.

The Wrath struck first in the 15th minute, converting a header deep inside the Royals' box. Moments later, the lights came on, illuminating the continuous problems the Royals faced in central defense.

With Gill sitting out after receiving the red card in the previous game against Delaware, it would have been an opportune time for the much-desired Steve Franzke to make his Royals debut. But the Royals were having a tough time convincing Franzke to sign for no money. So Gonzalo instead placed Chris Jones, normally an outside back, at sweeper.

"I thought his speed and ability to mark coming out of the back was better than anybody else," said Gonzalo. "He did very good."

Jones covered the area well, but many of his services out of the back were out of desperation, resulting in repeated lost possessions. Meanwhile, Simpson was serving up various-toned verbal shots from his position in front of the Royals' goal.

After Rachid Mahboub whiffed at a shot from the 18, following a brilliant individual run down half the field, Simpson yelled, "Kick the ball, Jesus Christ."

Minutes later, following a Royals' header on goal that went way wide, Simpson yelled, "My God," turned with agitation and walked back toward the Royals' goal, dropping his arms in disgust.

He chattered constantly to his defenders when the ball was near the Royals' goal, directing players to proper positions and commenting on their play. "You gotta check harder to that," he said once to a Royals defender.

Simpson kept the Royals in the game with two superb saves late in the first half. With about five minutes remaining, a Wrath player sprinted toward goal ahead of the defense. Simpson ran to the top of the box and deflected the shot high and forward as he fell. A couple of minutes later, Simpson sprinted out to the box to clear a long ball with a scissors kick, narrowly beating a Wrath attacker about 25 yards out from goal.

The late barrage by the Wrath placed Gonzalo in a tizzy. He was the most irate I had ever seen him at the beginning of the half time talk.

"I don't have a fucking idea what we're trying to do," he yelled.

Suddenly, Gonzalo collected himself for a brief moment of composure. He did not want his language to offend the younger fans.

"Are there any kids around?" he said quietly, as he quickly scoured the area.

No kids, so he continued.

"Is this the first time we've ever played? There's no creation up front. And there are too many coaches out there. I'm tired of that. I don't want to hear anything from anybody on the field."

Trying to instill more imagination up front, Gonzalo substituted Leonardo Thiombiano, a former member of the Washington Mustangs, for Mahboub at half time. It was Thiombiano's first appearance for the Royals. "We were not making Roanoke's defense work up front," said Gonzalo. "We were not doing anything up front."

Thiombiano is a pure goal scorer. He tallied seven goals in nine games for the Mustangs in 1996 and 16 goals in three years with the Burkina Faso National Team, from 1994 to 1996.

The 27-year-old started playing soccer professionally in Africa at age 16. From 1988 to 1996, he scored 150 goals in 244 matches for the Shooting Stars of Ougadougou, which won the African Champions Cup in 1992. Thiombiano showed during the Royals' preseason that he could be a potent offensive asset when he scored three goals in a preseason scrimmage against American University.

Thiombiano, a radio technician and journalist since 1991, arrived in the United States in June 1996 to learn about commercial radio in the U.S. and do some work for his father with the Voice of America (VOA). Thiombiano's father, Moustapha, a former professional pop musician who worked with Quincy Jones and The Jacksons when he lived in Los Angeles, in 1991 created the first independent radio network in Africa, Horizon-FM in Burkina Faso.

Thiombiano's work lasted only three weeks at VOA, but he stayed in the Washington area to play for the Mustangs and work as an art seller. After the Mustangs folded following the 1996 season, Thiombiano joined Iberia, Gonzalo's team in the NVSL. Thiombiano played on Gonzalo's Virginia State amateur team that won the Region I tournament in 1997 and finished second that year in the Donnelly Cup.

Thiombiano had trained with the Royals since preseason but confusion with management about his release from the Burkina Faso National Team delayed his debut with the Royals until the Roanoke game.

His radiant smile and endearing personality added a pleasant element to the Royals atmosphere. Many times he called me at home, wondering about my well-being and progress on the book.

At times, though, it seemed Thiombiano was too congenial on the field. His scoring prowess was in check against the Wrath. He did not muster one shot on goal and showed a low level of fitness.

By midway through the second half, most of the Royals players reflected Thiombiano's lack of effectiveness. Players, coaches and management were visibly frustrated.

Forward Leonardo Thiombiano made his Royals debut about midway through the season.

"These players are not fit," said Sheta, standing restlessly behind the Royals bench. "It's obvious the players can't make a commitment on their own time."

With about 20 minutes remaining and the Royals still down 1-0, assistant coach Matt Badiee yelled from the bench to Alberto Ogando to track back on defense after he got caught up in the Royals attacking third. Ogando, clearly fatigued, did not appreciate the command. "What the fuck?" he yelled, loud enough to be heard clearly in the stands. "It's called switching. Tony (Trepal) and I switched. Fuck you."

The players sat in stunned silence on the bench. Badiee, clearly miffed, did not retort. Perhaps the fact that Ogando and the Royals were not able to muster any real offensive attack all game fueled Ogando's frustration.

When the Wrath scored again some three minutes later, it was a collective punch to the guts of the Royals players. Their sterile attack continued to the end of the game, which the Royals lost, 2-0.

Some 10 minutes after the game, General Manager Sherif Shehata stormed into the somber locker room in a rage. "I'm sick and tired of listening to excuses," he yelled.

He then turned quickly towards the door and walked out, yelling "It sucks! It sucks!" his arms raised and face quivering.

Later, in the spacious hall outside the locker room, Gonzalo was perplexed. "Personally, I don't know what to do," he said. "I will tell you this. I need players this week and will need to release some players. I am sorry. I am feeling pressure. I don't know what to do, what to tell you."

A LOOSE FIT

I t was a couple days into June, about one week after my 40th birthday. Most of May had been a good month for me with the Royals. I finally started to feel like I fit in, physically and socially. After about two months of regular training, I had gained a level of fitness I had not felt since college some 20 years ago. My weight, usually around 175 pounds, had fallen to near 165 pounds (my college running weight was 150 pounds). My straight-away speed felt superb and in runs of 20 meters or longer, I kept pace with the rest of the boys. And I had forgotten how much fun regular soccer training could be. It was much more fun than running gut-wrenching track intervals on a regular basis.

It helped that much rain fell in April and May. This kept the ground soft and eased the impact on my aging bones, allowing me to train harder with more comfort. Up to that point, the only physical discomfort of concern I felt was a slight pain at the inside back of my left Achilles tendon. It happened every time my left leg hit the ground while jogging around the field before practice sometime in early May.

Socially, it seemed that the players had accepted the fact that I was going to be nosing around for awhile. Some seemed quite intrigued by what I was doing, a few others seemed suspicious and — what I found amazing —

a handful had no clue I was out there to write a book. They must have thought I was some delusional idiot going to practice almost every day and waiting naively for the coach to place me on a game roster.

After I asked the Royals management if I could write the book, neither they nor Gonzalo ever gathered the team around to explain my venture. Maybe they felt I was just another wannabe who was going to quit after a couple of weeks.

Anxiety surfaced on occasion. During a restless sleep in the early morning of June 3, I dreamed I scored two goals in a practice scrimmage. I converted one with a powerful header just inside the 18-yard line. It's funny how dreams can really distort reality. A powerful header usually requires strong jumping ability. As you get older, vertical jumps for a header are more like a hop in the general direction of the ball.

I remember most vividly, though, a goal I could not score. A ball was sent from the central midfield through the seam of a defense that had applied an off side trap. I got behind the defense just inside midfield and started chasing down the ball. I maintained my pace with the retreating defender as if I was half my age. The running felt effortless. But strangely, the field moved below in a broad blur as if I stayed in one position running on a treadmill.

No matter how hard I pushed, I could not catch up to the ball, which never slowed down and stayed teasingly only a couple steps ahead of me. It eventually rolled over the endline and out of my grasp. The keeper never came off his line, showing his indifference to my effort. I remember a mocking expression on his face. Was he ridiculing me for thinking I could maintain such a pace? Perhaps he realized I would never possess the ball.

The symbolism seemed evident. No matter how hard I tried to play catch up with soccer, the best opportunities had already passed me by.

I became comfortable with some aspects of being on the team. My level of play felt adequate. I felt most of the players accepted—and some even embraced—my presence. But from where was this anxiety originating? Were my goals with the Royals unrealistic? Was my subconscious telling me I was chasing something excessively elusive?

Still, my resolve remained firm to play in a professional soccer match. "Think 13."

TITLE GAME(S)

The Royals had ample time to mull over their pitiful performance against the Roanoke Wrath on June 13. Their next league match, a home contest against the South Carolina Shamrocks, fell 13 days following Gonzalo's promise to release players and bring in some fresh talent. After the loss to the Wrath, Gonzalo said the team would practice every day the following week. But the threat fell victim to Mother Nature's foul mood. Torrential rains during yet another violent afternoon thunderstorm forced practice to be moved inside on Monday. A handful of players, including myself, drove out to Lewinsville Park expecting a hard practice despite the rain that started falling.

We made the mistake of not checking the players' voice mail recording that all season long told of any last-minute changes. Practice was taking place at Mo Sheta's indoor soccer complex at least an arduous hour away from Lewinsville during rush hour traffic, and the message told of an important team meeting. The impending venture proved too formidable for the few of us who showed up at the park for practice. Instead, while deciding whether or not to work out on our own, a few of us stood in the light rain in the parking lot while Chris Jones sat comfortably in his adidas-emblazoned van, chatting about the team's woes.

Jones talked with typical good-natured passion. "Silvino has always had enough good players to not have to coach too much. He would just let them play," he said.

Thunder and lightning soon joined the stormy mix and the rain pelted us with greater intensity.

The topic soon turned to contracts and money. Jones and Vigon said they were asked to sign three-year contracts with the Royals, but they declined.

"Who's gonna sign a three-year contract for no money?" said Jones, his voice rising to an excited pitch.

"I'd do it if they paid me $150 a game, but not for nothing," said Vigon.

Eventually, two players, Mohamed Kaba and Jeff Cullina, stayed to play with about a dozen or so other diehards who had formed a pick up game of their own. Cullina, a scrappy player who showed as much heart as any player in practice, worked out with the Royals much of the season to stay fit for the upcoming college season at Virginia Tech. He did not sign a contract so he could retain his amateur status to play college ball.

Kaba, a former member of the U-17 National Team of Guinea, had trained with the Royals since the beginning of the regular season. Gonzalo badly wanted Kaba to play for the Royals, but Kaba had trouble getting a release from his native country's federation.

Meanwhile, most of the team showed up at the indoor practice. The environment was dry, but equally as electric as storm-soaked Lewinsville Park.

The meeting took place after a fitness session followed by some light ball work. During the meeting, management handed out a questionnaire that asked the players' expectations of the coaches, the other players and the organization, their own personal goals and expectations and how they kept fit away from team practice.

Matt Ferry, one of the players more loyal to Gonzalo, voiced the most displeasure during the meeting, complaining mostly about a lack of team professionalism.

Ferry, a broad-shouldered, tall, bruising central midfielder imparts a classic Norwegian presence with short, light blond hair, a solid chin and a sturdy stare. He has had great success with teams coached by Gonzalo. Ferry earned Most Valuable Player honors at the 1996 National Amateur Cup, won by his team, Iberia, and was captain of the 1997 Virginia State team. Also in 1997, he played for the East team that won the U.S. Soccer Festival.

Ferry, 25, had already proved that he was not shy about voicing an opinion. At the beginning of a practice in early June, he became frustrated with some drills. The practice began with a small game of five-on-five while some other players stood around watching. The Royals had just lost two consecutive games, the most recent a 4-1 loss to the Delaware Wizards. An uneasy mood hovered over the practice.

"What is the purpose of this drill?" Ferry firmly asked of assistant coach Matt Badiee. "Is this something we really need to be working on?"

"Everything we do has a purpose," replied Badiee, with conviction.

During a team chat before a game later in the season, Ferry offered some advice about a subtle defensive tactic that bordered on offensive. "If you're hanging on to (an opponent's) shirt, they're not going to call it," he said. "Just hang on and pull them down."

His no-nonsense approach to the game was evident during a candid conversation we had about the team meeting.

"Our biggest complaint was that the practices weren't professional enough," he said. "We seemed to play tough, but then we'd lose games with the same things. For example, we'd get beat on off side traps. We never worked on that in practice. And we have good size on this team; but, up to that point, we had never worked on free kicks in practice. I said 'A team is as professional as the organization,' and the organization is amateur."

Ferry has spent most of his life in Washington, D.C. He was born in Georgetown and moved to Bethesda, Maryland when he was 13. Ferry played on Maryland ODP teams each year from ages 12 to 18.

One of Ferry's youth club teams was the Potomac Mustangs, coached by John Kerr, Sr. when Kerr also coached the Washington Stars of the old American Soccer League. When he was 16, Ferry practiced often with the Stars. Also at 16, Ferry started playing for the Spartans in the NVSL. He later switched over to play for Iberia and Gonzalo.

After graduating from high school, Ferry tried a professional soccer career in England. He trained with apprentice and reserve teams for third division Leyton Orient in the East end of London. The team paid some living and training expenses while Ferry trained with them full-time and went to school part time.

"I wanted to see how far I could go with soccer in England," he said.

After two years in England, Ferry returned to the U.S. and chose to attend George Washington University with a full soccer scholarship.

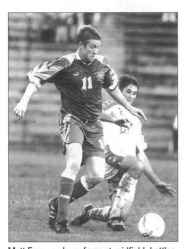

Ferry survived a life-threatening experience during the summer before his sophomore season at George Washington. He and a soccer playing friend spent two months that summer training with a second division professional team in Chile. Ferry started feeling sick about halfway through the trip. He could not sleep for more than 25 minutes without having to urinate and his eyesight starting failing. He had a constant, craving thirst. "I thought it was because we were working out all the time in a desert environment," he said.

Matt Ferry, a clever force at midfield, battles diabetes while he seeks a pro career.

Ferry's body crashed with only three days remaining in the trip. By that time, he had lost about 40 pounds.

"I had no energy," he said. "I couldn't do anything." He returned to the U.S. and spent one week in the hospital, where it was determined he had diabetes.

Health problems continued. Two weeks later, he woke up one morning with a sore ankle. By the end of the day, the ankle swelled up so severely he could walk only with crutches. The discomfort soon spread to the other ankle and then both knees. He woke up some mornings with his eyes crusted shut. He was urinating blood and developed urethritis.

"One doctor thought I got a venereal disease while I was in South America," he said.

Ferry had developed rheumatoid arthritis and was told he would never play soccer again. He could not run for seven months. But Ferry was determined to maintain some physical conditioning. He went to a swimming pool daily to jog in the water. And after one year he returned to playing the game he loved.

Once back on the field, he helped lead George Washington to winning records in two of their next three seasons. But it was not enough to forge a lasting pleasant feeling.

"I never really enjoyed my time at G.W.," said Ferry, a three-time captain of the Colonials. "It wasn't that good a team and our facilities were shit."

Ferry finished his college career in 1997 and started playing with the Royals soon after. By that time, he had developed a routine to monitor his diabetes while playing soccer.

He tests his blood sugar level before and during half time of every game, and sometimes after a game. Ferry pricks a finger to draw a drop of blood. He places the blood on a slide that is inserted into a device that digitally reads his blood sugar level. If it reads low, he'll eat a banana, bread or a sports bar, or drink a large quantity of Gatorade.

"I always feel better in the second half," said Ferry. "If I have too much or too little sugar, I feel sluggish. By the second half I burn off the sugar."

Ferry says if a diabetic must choose between high or low blood sugar levels, they should choose high. Blood sugar levels too-low can result in blacking out or a diabetic-induced coma.

"Sometimes it's tough on the road because you don't always know what time you're going to eat or what you're going to eat," he said.

Ferry's elevated sugar level almost forced him out of a Royals game on the road against the South Carolina Shamrocks. Before the game, Ferry let his blood sugar level get too high.

"I felt real bad during the game and probably should not have played," he said. "After the game, I felt like I was going to die. I probably should have gone to a hospital emergency room. I was probably too stubborn about staying in the game. I've told myself that I would never let the diabetes be an excuse for me not to play a game. But it's not worth the risk. I learned a valuable lesson from that game."

Ferry also learned a lot about the realities of minor league soccer in the U.S. during the Royals' first season. One of the more revealing lessons revolved around financial concerns on the team.

"I know you have to make money to pay people," he said. "But the money was constantly left in the balance. The first time I heard we weren't getting paid was during the New England trip (in early May). Before the season, I was thinking of moving. If I had known that, I might not be here.

"That night (at the team meeting), they made a mistake. They threatened that players would be released if we don't play better. But two weeks later, nobody's gone. That's an idle threat.

"I knew it would be this way, more of an NVSL all-star team than a USISL team. But the teams we play against, the other players aren't that much better; they're much smarter."

At practice the day after the meeting, the weather had cleared but the tail of the team storm still wagged faintly. Gonzalo gathered his tattered troops in a circle before the practice. Rick Engelfried, the team captain, tried to keep the team pumped up.

"At the beginning of the season, it seemed to be the consensus of the team — starting with Mo and including all the players — that our goal was to make the playoffs," he said. "Right now, that doesn't look too good. But let's start with it today. Let's see if we can turn it around."

Engelfried had mostly been a background, non-verbal leader of this team, inspiring more with his impassioned and aggressive

Rick Engelfried was the most versatile player for the Royals.

play than with his rhetoric. He dispatched the pre-practice speech with a tentativeness that seemed to border on reluctance. But, typical of the fighter he is, Engelfried delivered when he felt the team needed it most.

Engelfried, 29, began playing soccer at age five and has spent his entire soccer life in Virginia. A native of Washington, D.C., Engelfried played club soccer for the Reston Warriors and Braddock Road Cardinals, both in Northern Virginia. He was a member of the U-17 and U-19 Virginia ODP teams and was a star at South Lakes High School in Reston. Engelfried departed James Madison University as one of the top goal scorers in the school's history with 38 career goals. After college, he played club ball for Mo's Sports Shop and Total Fitness. A computer software engineering consultant, Engelfried hopes someday to play in the A-League.

Gonzalo ended the prepractice team chat session in typical fiery form. "As a group, I don't think we're thinking the same way," he said. "Let's see if we can work together. If somebody doesn't like that, then you must leave."

Nobody left. But at least one player was moved by the moody oratory. Minutes later the team circled for its typical, prepractice stretch following a five-minute jog. Standing with legs spread, casually stretching his groin muscles, Steve Gill, lightheartedly challenged Engelfried.

"We need you to be Dunga," he said.

Engelfried laughed calmly, understanding the reference to the moody central midfielder who anchored the Brazilian midfield with his hard, heady play and his controversial method of verbally berating players during a game, no matter the status of the player or the size of the audience.

Dunga was in Gill's mind because earlier that day Dunga nearly chewed off the cheeks of forward Bebeto during Brazil's preliminary round match against Morocco in the World Cup, with a worldwide audience of probably one billion people watching.

It was difficult to imagine Engelfried enjoying a similar meal at the expense of one of his players, especially in public view. After practice, though, Engelfried did munch on a little introspective fat about the previous day's meeting and the team's lack of success.

He sat comfortably on the ground and talked calmly, staring mostly straight ahead, his arms across the top of his bent knees with one hand grasping the opposite wrist.

"The purpose of the meeting was to air out opinions and to talk about what's wrong with the team, to find anything that would help the team improve," he said. "Mo reiterated that communication on the field was nonexistent. And we are still trying to figure out our style. Should we be a possession type of team and kick the ball around? What kind of runs should players make? We didn't do walk-throughs at practice to determine where players should be in relation to the ball.

"(Assistant coach) Matt (Badiee) said the most passes we strung together in the game last Saturday was five. Mo and Silvino said we play with a lack of heart and effort, that five or six guys play hard and that others, after making a mistake, hang their heads."

"Do you see that?" I asked.

"Yeah, sometimes I do," he said. "It's frustrating for me as a captain because people ask me to talk to the players and tell them to do this and that, and then they don't. After a while, I get the attitude, 'Why bother?' I get quite frustrated sometimes. Some players don't listen to the coach. It's a matter of respect.

"And then I have to think about my game. I watched a lot of German league games when I was young and I try to impose that style. If the coach says something at practice, everybody should do it. They're trying to get everybody on the same page for one common goal."

"Can the problems be attributed to this being the team's first year?" I asked.

"If we were to play games like we did against New Hampshire and Charlotte—we busted our butts, got a few bad breaks, but we walked off the field knowing we gave it 100 percent—if we were losing games like that and were still at 3-9, yeah, we could use that excuse," he said. "But we're not."

The frustration in Engelfried's voice reached a level of fervor.

"We've got guys making stupid mistakes," he said. "Most of these guys have played division one college soccer and they're making elementary mistakes. Sure, we've had problems with the organization itself—the way our trips are handled, some problems with uniforms. You can make excuses for them since it's our first year. But not how we've been playing."

"Is it a matter of personnel or attitude?" I asked.

"It's a little bit of both," he said. "We haven't been creating a lot of chances. Maybe we should put someone else up front and change the formation a bit."

Engelfried, the great goal scorer in college who had played only sparingly as a striker for the Royals, was unaware of the clairvoyance of his words.

The cavernous home locker room for the Royals, used primarily by athletic teams and gym classes at Fairfax High School, promoted no sense of identity for the team. The hundreds of metal lockers are bolted in dozens of rows in a room as long and wide as a basketball court. The airy, generic room could comfortably accommodate two college football teams.

Still, an intimate feeling enveloped the pregame chat for the game against the South Carolina Shamrocks on June 26. The team sat in the back left corner on wooden benches that protrude from the bases of the lockers. They surrounded Gonzalo, whose words echoed through the room for impact.

Gonzalo spoke calmly, his message laced with a sense of humor, as he drew player positions on a hand-held board.

"This is a championship game for us," he said. "We have nine games left. Starting tonight, we must win games to make the playoffs."

He paused and cracked a wry smile, signaling levity.

"If we lose, we will have a meeting on Monday about how bad the coach was," he said. He chuckled, placing the players at relative ease. "I see what's happening in the papers," he said.

The previous day, the U.S. Men's National Team had lost its final first round game in the World Cup to Yugoslavia, securing a winless campaign for the Americans and prompting a verbal media attack against its leader, Steve Sampson.

"When we defend, everybody has to defend," he said. "We want forwards to come back. If we don't, we tend to have too much gap in the middle. When I say something from the bench, I don't want anybody talking back."

Not much more was said in the locker room. The players departed with a clearly defined mission. This was the big one. Another loss could be devastating.

As I walked down the bleachers into the bowl that was their stadium, I spotted Mark Simpson sitting cozily about 10 rows up with his petite and pretty girlfriend, Tammy. Game time was about 30 minutes away. My first thought was, "I bet Mark could never do that before a D.C. United game."

Imagine that scene with Bruce Arena peering up from the field, summoning his keeper to the field for warm-up.

"C'mon, Mark, cut it out. We need you to come down here and warm up Scott (Garlick) and Tom (Presthus)."

Unfortunately for Simpson, at the time, that would not have been an unlikely command from Arena. He had not seen one minute of action with United all season.

I had developed a comfortable friendship with Simpson while working for D.C. United. We are both avid golfers and managed to play a couple of rounds together. As he recovered from the knee injury, we talked often about his rehabilitation, and, for the most part, his spirits had remained high despite repeated setbacks.

But while we chatted idly a few minutes later, I first noticed his frustration about not playing for United this season. He said his knee had been ready for some time and Arena had promised him he would play. Still, he wondered if he would play for United again. Minutes later he walked casually onto the field and warmed up with evident lethargy.

Gonzalo would need Simpson's sense of assuredness in goal since, for the first time, he was starting 21-year-old Stephen Franzke as a central defender along with Steve Gill.

Franzke, who finished his career at American University the previous fall, had been training with the Royals off and on for a little more than one month. He enjoyed a stellar career at American and started every game he played, totaling more than 80 matches. He was an All-South Atlantic Region pick his senior year, during which American was ranked as high as fifth in the country and advanced to the NCAA Tournament quarterfinals.

Since May, Gonzalo had pleaded repeatedly to Royals management to sign Franzke. But, Franzke had avoided signing a contract because the Royals could not offer money. His Royals career lasted one game, and it did not create good memories.

Franzke played primarily as a sweeper, replacing Engelfried, who moved up to forward. Gill, who had been playing mostly as a sweeper, moved up to stopper.

As he walked from the locker room to the field, Franzke was asked if he planned to play in a flat back-four.

"I don't know," he said. "Even if (Gonzalo) wants that, I'll be dropping back."

Another first-time starter for the Royals was Mark Vita, a fleet-footed and clever-mouthed spark of energy who is more comfortable going forward. In his debut for the Royals, he scored the team's only goal in an exhibition against the Bolivian U-19 National Team on June 21, five days before the Shamrocks game. Vita, a graduate of Fairfax High School, had completed his eligibility at George Mason University that fall.

Vita is dynamic, elusive and a blitzkrieg in the first 30 meters. At George Mason, he started 21 of 22 games his senior year and showed consistent, if not explosive, offensive numbers. He scored seven goals in both his junior and senior years and also had four and five assists, respectively.

Vita's personality is nearly as potent as his playing style. He is the consummate wisecracker, a gregarious grunger. At times, when pushed, he talked dreamily about competing on the professional Jet Ski circuit. When not working at a soccer camp last summer, several times he spent much of the summer day at Lake Occoquan riding a Jet Ski before he arrived at practice.

Vita's chiding and cavorting kept the mood light during practices and his devilish smile often signaled that something was up. His strong sense of humor was contagious.

Soon after Vita joined the team, I gave the players a sheet on which to provide background information for the book. A couple of Vita's responses reflected his flip, almost defiant, approach to serious matters.

Question: Family? (wife, kids)

Response: None that I know of.

Question: Why did you want to play for the Royals?

Response: After college I took some time off to relax. I missed soccer and I was getting fat.

Question: What are your goals in soccer; any other professional/career goals?

Response: 1) to have fun; 2) to get Dave in a game (a reference to my desire to play a game with the Royals); 3) to play at the highest level I can; 4) marry rich.

You may get the impression that Vita did not approach soccer with sufficient seriousness. Not true. George Mason Head Coach Gordon Bradley remembers that, for awhile, Vita took the game too seriously. His strong personality blossomed toward the end of his college career. "In his first years, he was kind of overshadowed by other players," said Bradley. "But by his senior year, his personality developed. He's a witty person."

On the field, Bradley feels Vita has the tools to eventually play in MLS, which is Vita's goal. "Mark is probably the hardest shot maker I've had at George Mason University," he said. "And he had a quality of aggression (in his final season) that was stronger than his previous years. He kind of took it upon himself to be a leader on the field."

Vita ultimately proved himself very goal-worthy and infused the team with energy and personality at midfield. By the end of the season—despite joining the team nearly two months into the campaign—Vita led the team in scoring with seven goals.

Vita started his first league match with the Royals against the Shamrocks at central midfield on the right side next to flank midfielder Tim Prisco.

And he profoundly validated his placement on the starting 11 within the first 10 minutes. In the ninth minute, he took a restart from the right flank about 10 yards short of midfield.

A few Royals set up in a straight line just outside the 18-yard box. As Vita started the ball toward the near post, Engelfried, one of the taller players on the field, began his run to goal.

The ball curved toward the onrushing Engelfried, who timed his jump perfectly, beat a defender to the ball and headed it emphatically inside the upper right corner of the goal. Engelfried reacted with a perfunctory, primal scream while he continued his run toward the near touchline. But his score surprisingly prompted little exuberance from the meager crowd, or even the players on the bench. The relative quiet at the stadium returned quickly.

The irony of the Royals scoring their first goal off a restart was conspicuous to only a few. The team spent a solid hour working on restarts two days after the loss to the Wrath. It was the first time all season that the team had done so in practice.

The second portion of the first half took on a familiar look for the Royals. Franzke had practiced only a few times with the Royals. Confusion reigned in central defense, a sign of unfamiliarity between Franzke and regular starters Gill and Vigon. The Shamrocks started to wreak havoc along the Royals' defensive back four, requiring Simpson to respond with several heroic saves.

Despite his vow to retreat, Franzke was pushing forward far enough to boil Gonzalo's blood. Gonzalo yelled vehemently to Franzke a couple of times from the bench.

"Steve! Franzke! Drop back. A few yards. Drop back."

In the 33rd minute a Shamrock player dispossessed Vita just outside the Royals' box as the Royals' defense attempted to push up and build an attack. The player dribbled directly on goal, sent the ball across the goal mouth and past an onrushing Simpson to another Shamrock player, who tapped the ball in to tie the match at one.

A couple minutes later further confusion between Franzke and outside defender Vigon nearly led to another Shamrock goal. Both played a 50-50 ball tentatively, failing to communicate their intentions, as a Shamrock player stepped in between them, took possession of the ball and shot just wide of the net.

When Vigon muttered frustrating words to Franzke, Steve Gill had seen and heard enough. He yelled at both players while walking downfield.

"Hey, you," he said pointing to Franzke, "Talk to him. Adam, shut up."

Vigon walked tentatively back to his defensive position, his head down. "He's fuckin' up, Gilly," he said.

Gonzalo had displayed some serious temper tantrums during previous half time speeches. But in the Shamrocks game, his anger brewed beyond the boiling point.

Gonzalo addressed the team behind one of the goals at the end of the field. Simpson, sitting on the track surrounding the field, listened from the back of the group as Gonzalo began by lamenting about poor man-marking in the final 20 minutes of the first half.

"Not this half time speech again," Simpson said quietly and with dismay.

Gonzalo was yelling loud enough to make inaudible Simpson's remark. The F- word became his most favored, and overused, epithet.

His most impassioned point was a reference to the team meeting. "Two weeks ago, you fucking criticized me and you go and fucking do this now," he said. "I want real soccer, with pride. I am embarrassed now."

Gonzalo then walked away slowly, a pained man who sensed his mood needed to be tempered. A more composed Sheta soon stepped in and tried to calm his players.

"Let's go out with a positive approach," he said. "Let's make sure we cover for our men."

As the team gathered back at the bench to start the second half, Gill tried to infuse a heavier challenge. "I'm sick of being told what to do and when to do it," he said forcefully. "Let's see if you can take this like a man. And don't take it personally."

Vita was apologetic as the team dispersed to start the second half.

"Sorry about that last goal, guys," he said, with humility. "I should have cleared it out."

The game against the Shamrocks was the Royals' sixth home game. And although they were drawing around 200 a game, a handful of spectators had formed a small and consistently loyal cheering section.

The Royals had also attracted a vocal and regular heckler named John Stafford from Alexandria, Virginia. Stafford is a D.C. United season ticket holder with his wife and is a member of that team's fan club, the Screaming Eagles. He was not much of a soccer fan until D.C. United came to town. Now he calls himself a "die-hard" fan.

Stafford was the only fan at the game wearing a Royals team jersey, which he bought for $45. He said he attends Royals games because "it gives him an appreciation for the skill level at D.C. United games."

He was asked if he really cared about the Royals. "If the Royals start winning, I might start caring," he said. Stafford later said he decided to attend the Shamrocks game because "it beats sitting at home watching TV."

Where's his wife?

"Royals games are too nerdy for her," he said.

Stafford's verbal antics echoed throughout the stadium loudly enough to be heard across the field. About midway through the second half, he registered his most profound offering.

"You guys are playing against a shamrock. What's a shamrock? Something a cow eats!"

The Shamrocks' second year coach, Leo Flanagan, a true Irishman, took offense to the remark belittling the symbol of his motherland. He turned toward Stafford and flashed a brief, irritated stare. That seemed to encourage Stafford even more.

"A shamrock is just a marshmallow I pull out of my box of Lucky Charms," he yelled to the Royals. "How can you get beat by a marshmallow?"

The heckling seemed to help place Flanagan on an emotional edge. With about six minutes remaining and the Shamrocks clinging to a 2-1 lead following a score off a corner kick, Royals assistant John Ormassa, sitting on the midfield side of the Royals bench, noticed that Flanagan had been continuously crossing the midfield line into the Royals' side of the field. He complained to the fourth official that Flanagan was "outside his technical area."

"You shut your fuckin' mouth," Flanagan yelled toward Ormassa.

The clovered lads endured all the hostility and hung on for a gritty 2-1 win. Flanagan was not done, though, when the final whistle blew.

As he walked off the field, he looked up toward Stafford and said, "Hey, you know what a Shamrock is now?" Stafford did not respond, but the mostly mild-mannered Sheta, standing behind the Royals bench, did.

"Don't be talking like that to our fans," he sternly said to Flanagan.

Flanagan said nothing in return, apparently content that his team had handed the Royals their fourth consecutive loss.

A home match against the Myrtle Beach SeaDawgs scheduled two days after the Shamrocks game was rained out. The Royals did not play again until July 8 — two weeks after the loss to the Shamrocks — when they hosted the Wilmington Hammerheads. They could not have asked for a more suitable opponent. The Wilmington Hammerheads arrived in Northern Virginia for a Wednesday night match losers of two games within a three-day span the previous weekend. They had fallen back to sixth place, six points ahead of the Royals for the last playoff spot.

Gonzalo clearly understood the severity of the match. His pregame speech in the locker room rang of familiarity.

"This is a playoff game for us," he said. "We had a good week of practice. We've had some arguments, some good. Sometimes arguing is good. This is the championship final for us."

Eight games remained on the schedule, so perhaps his tone was a touch melodramatic. Gonzalo's urgency was ignited by a bit of confusion about how many teams qualify for the playoffs. Before the game, he and most players thought only the top four teams from their division advanced to the playoffs, but the top six of the eight division teams would qualify for post-season play.

Still, a loss against the struggling Hammerheads could send the Royals, enmeshed in a four-game losing streak with a 4-11 record, into a psychological quagmire.

They seemed destined for the depths of the despaired after falling behind 2-0 after 11 minutes. But Gonzalo's normally short fuse never went ablaze. Instead, he made one of his best coaching decisions of the season. Engelfried admittedly had been struggling in practice the couple days prior to the match because of an injured hamstring. At the beginning of practice the day before the game, Gonzalo called over his five key, but hampered, players—Engelfried, Trepal, Mahboub, Kerns and Ferry—into a circle and asked them if they were okay to play the next day.

"If you can't, you need to be honest with me," he said. "This game is too important."

Not surprisingly, all said they were fit to start. But Gonzalo felt Engelfried was favoring the hamstring in the Wilmington match. After the game, Engelfried said the leg felt fine, but he clearly was not his typical aggressive self on the front line.

With about 25 minutes remaining in the first half, Gonzalo subbed Thiombiano for Engelfried, who walked to the bench with a look of consternation. But Engelfried, the team captain, reacted with a positive perspective, slapping a teammate's hand or two as he sat down on the bench.

Engelfried did not get an answer from Gonzalo about his early dismissal until the end of half time as they walked to the bench. Moments later,

Gonzalo explained the decision.

"He's hurt," he said. "There was no pressure in the back. I told him I trust him, if you want to play, you start. But he was not applying pressure."

The Royals played the next 10 minutes as if they had taken a time-release pill that combated soccer impotency. Thiombiano, speedier than Engelfried, scored the Royals' first goal within five minutes of entering the match. Rachid Mahboub, looking like he had finally grown comfortable with the left midfield flank position, developed the play with a confident and aggressive individual run down the left side. Racing past a defender, he took the ball to the end line before sending a weedkiller across the goal mouth, where Thiombiano slid onto the ball and poked it into the goal from about five yards out.

The Royals tied the match three minutes later, in the 28th minute. The vibrant Vita collected a throw-in just inside the left side of the box, and after a defender fell down on the rain-soaked field, he had more time to compose himself and rip a left-footed shot into the back of the net from about 12 yards away.

Just three minutes later, Thiombiano collected a deflected pass in the Hammerheads backfield, raced toward goal and fired a rocket from just inside the box that was deflected away nicely by the Hammerheads keeper. But Vita, standing just outside the box to the left, took advantage of the convenient carom and one-timed another left-footed blast for another score. The Royals led 3-2 at half time.

The offensive flurry prompted one of the more relaxed half time speeches of the season by Gonzalo. He calmly asked for simple touches, more shooting and more aggression at midfield. He congratulated the team for a "great comeback."

"It's very important in the beginning of the second half that we keep up the pressure," he said. "We will dictate what happens."

Gill cautioned his teammates about complacency.

"Let's not think that we've won it," he said. "We've got 45 minutes left."

Vigon, a possessor of sharp wit, supported Gill's warning with a cynical commentary audible to only the few standing near him.

"Fuckin, ay'," he said with a chuckle. "This is the Royals."

The Royals failed to heed Gonzalo's call to dictate the pace early in the second half and almost allowed the Hammerheads to tie the match within the first few minutes. John Pascarella, starting in goal for the first time in four games, masterfully stuffed a 1 v 1 chance by Wilmington, setting the tone for a strong 45-minute performance.

The Royals then seemed to clinch the match after Mahboub scored in the 55th minute following another outstanding individual effort. He craftily controlled a free kick from midfield just inside the box, moved a few steps to his right and shot a blast back towards the far post. The score capped an effort by Mahboub that warranted "Player of the Match" honors, if one was given. He controlled the left flank with artistic abandon, weaving around and through defenders and winning most 50-50 balls.

About five minutes after Mahboub put the Royals ahead 4-2, Gonzalo made a peculiar substitution that threatened to override his masterful first-half decision and placed the cheery Royals bench into a bit of a funk.

Maxx Henry-Frazier, at 19 the youngest member of the team, had played sparingly for the Royals all season. He usually entered a match when the Royals needed an offensive spark. When he checked in at the fourth officials' table between the benches, I wondered why Gonzalo had ordered him in. Standing behind the table, I wished him good luck.

He turned to me with a confused expression and said, "I'm playing sweeper." His unsolicited information seemed a result of wanting to share his surprise with someone before he entered the match.

Henry-Frazier is a solid midfielder and forward. The Royals player with perhaps the most promising professional future, he had hoped to be playing for a developmental club somewhere in Europe, by the time the Hammerheads came north to Northern Virginia.

Henry-Frazier is quick and graceful with a controlled sense of flair. He learned the game with stern dedication at an early age, playing most of his early years with the Alexandria Soccer Association. By the time he was 11 years old, Henry-Frazier had spent two years training, mostly seven days a week, with a former professional player from Peru. They practiced on tennis courts when it snowed. The coach missed just one day in two years, after he cut off the tip of his finger.

"People said they would burn out, but I said so what, if you burn out, do something else," said his father, John Henry-Frazier as he watched an early season practice.

Maxx Henry-Frazier did not burn out. In fact, he flourished. When he was 13, Henry-Frazier played with Saprisa, a local amateur team made up primarily of El Salvadorans.

"He was 17 for about four years," said John Henry-Frazier, with a chuckle. "As long as you said you were 17, you could play. The league knew he was 13, but he tried to keep it quiet with the players because we weren't sure if they would let him play. Then he got an assist in a scrimmage and they signed him up in a parking lot. He started every game, even when he was four-foot-nine. It basically helped him to play quicker."

Until he was actually 17, Henry-Frazier joined his youth club team for weekend morning games in the National Capital Soccer League, a top area youth league, and played with the amateurs in the afternoon.

Henry-Frazier missed all but four games with his high school team, Lake Braddock, his senior year to try out with a reserve team with Nantes, a top professional club in France. In the summer of 1997, he won the U-18 U. S. Youth Soccer Association national title with Columbia (Maryland) City United.

The following fall, Henry-Frazier was a non-scholarship freshman starter at outside midfield for the University of Connecticut. He departed Connecticut after one semester and returned to Northern Virginia to prepare for tryouts with a couple of professional teams in Holland, including Wilhelm II. He had received hints that he would be invited to Holland during the summer of 1998.

While he sought soccer work abroad, Henry-Frazier planned to play with top amateur teams in the Washington, D.C. area. He attended an open tryout for the Royals and made the team. He found out about the tryout from his dad, who met someone on the street when both were walking their dogs.

"We started talking about soccer and he told me about a Royals tryout that was coming up," said John Henry-Frazier.

Henry-Frazier ultimately got his wish to play soccer abroad, but not in Europe. On October 13, he flew to Argentina to join a soccer school run by Rosario, a first division team in Argentina. He learned about the school from an official with Toluca, a top Mexican professional team.

Juan Gomez, a junior varsity coach at Wakefield High School in Arlington, Virginia who is well connected in the Hispanic soccer community in the Washington, D.C. area and in South America, first saw Henry-Frazier play while he was in high school. He tried then to convince him to play youth soccer in Mexico.

"We didn't know anything about it so we just ignored it," said John Henry-Frazier.

When Toluca was in Washington in September to play in the CONCACAF Champions Cup, Gomez took Maxx Henry-Frazier to see the official from Toluca. The official said they only consider Mexican players, but he suggested Henry-Frazier call a representative from the school in Rosario.

In the fall of 1998, Henry-Frazier lived in a townhouse in Rosario with four Spanish-speaking players. The players at the Rosario school make up its reserve teams.

"Maxx said they play soccer four hours a day and then watch it on television for the other 20 hours," said John Henry-Frazier, who pays $300 a month for Maxx's room and board. Maxx retained his amateur status so he could return to college in the fall of 1999, hopefully at St.

Maxx Henry-Frazier, the youngest Royal, showed much flair and promise.

Louis University. That is, of course, if he does not sign a professional contract in South America. Henry-Frazier has already been invited to try out with a first division club in the Bolivian professional league. He proved to be a fast-learning student at Rosario, scoring two goals in his first game with the reserve team.

But playing for the Royals against the Hammerheads in early July, Henry-Frazier was not asked to score any goals. His job was to defend.

No one was more miffed at the substitution than Gill, who had been playing sweeper. After he realized he was leaving the game, he walked slowly toward the bench with a look of sheer bewilderment.

"That's a stupid fuckin' sub," he muttered as he walked across the touchline. By that time he had taken off his team jersey in disgust.

Gonzalo sensed the displeasure building within Gill, who walked around the bench and reached for his bag. "That's it, Steve, leave the bench," he said calmly.

Within a minute, Gill walked quietly and hastily towards the locker-room.

Later, Gonzalo explained why he had subbed out one of his most loyal players. "He got a yellow card on the play right before I took him out," he said. "If I had kept him in the game, I knew he was going to get a red card. He knew why he was coming out."

If Gill had received a red card, he would have received at least a one-game suspension. "We were winning, but I was pissed off at different things in the game, at different players and my play," said Gill. "I can see his point of view. But we've played together for years. He should know I don't get too bad. It's either a red card the first time or just one yellow card."

With Gill out of the game, Gonzalo was relying on a player who had last played sweeper about seven years ago to anchor the Royals' defense. Henry-Frazier last played that position with a U-13 team in a Maryland State Cup final. Further, Henry-Frazier had not played that position in practice all season with the Royals. And it showed. He continuously wandered from the middle and pushed too far forward, prompting Gonzalo to remind him where to play. One time he yelled instructions in excited and unintelligible English obscured with a heavy Spanish accent. Badiee, sensing that Henry-Frazier did not understand the command, calmly followed up Gonzalo's command with a simple directive.

"Play the area between the posts," he yelled clearly.

Gonzalo later explained that he put Henry-Frazier in as sweeper because of his speed and good touch on the ball. Although mostly out of position, Henry-Frazier played skillfully and aggressively and helped the Royals withstand heavy pressure from the Hammerheads in the final 10 minutes to preserve the win.

While signing a shirt for a young fan after the game, Henry-Frazier was asked how it felt playing sweeper.

"Like it was the U-13 State Cup final," he said with a laugh. "I just kept saying, 'Get the ball out, get the ball out.' "

The final minutes of the game featured some ancillary drama. Pascarella felt that a referee assistant missed an off side call with about six minutes remaining and let him know about it. He directed a nearly 30-second, obscene verbal tirade to the referee that could be heard clearly on the Royals bench and in the stands.

To the assistant referee's credit, he initially allowed Pascarella to vent his anger without responding. But the assistant simply waited for the right moment to retaliate. He had noticed that a Royals equipment assistant was filling up small plastic water jugs and delivering them to Pascarella. During one attempt, the referee halted the hydration project in progress.

"Don't fill that up more than one quarter," the referee yelled to the assistant as he ran along the touchline away from the Royals bench to follow a play. "One quarter, or I'll pour it out."

Rick Engelfried heard the referee's command from the bench. He quickly complained to the fourth official, who tried to persuade the Royals bench to ignore it and let the game run out. Within a couple minutes, Gonzalo, who had been watching intently as his team battled a barrage of attempts on the Royals' goal, was told about the restriction.

In typical Gonzalo fashion, he managed to inject a little levity into a potentially tense situation. "What if he has a kidney problem?" he said with a conniving, boyish smile. "What do we do then?"

The Royals bench laughed and the situation was diffused. Gonzalo did not care to create turmoil as the Royals were closing in on an extraordinary moment. They were about to wrap up their most convincing and significant win of the season, a win that ended the longest losing streak of the year at four games, improved their record to 5-11 and placed them within three points of a playoff spot with seven games remaining.

For the first time in months, an opposing team felt the agony of defeat.

"God, we fuckin' suck," said a Hammerheads player to himself as he walked trudgingly off the field, the darkness of night covering him in despair. "I'm getting tired of this."

TAKING ONE MORE SHOT

The Royals practice started typically on June 25 with a casual warm-up jog around the field at Lewinsville Park in McLean, Virginia. But atypical was the presence of Scott Poirier, who had become an infrequent attendee at practice. And Poirier was struggling by the end of the first lap. "Man, I've lost all my fitness," he said, with labor. "That's what a day job does to you."

The season had started with much promise for Poirier. After he scored the winning goal in the final minute of overtime to beat the New Jersey Riptide in the season and home opener, it seemed the once-dominant Poirier would take full advantage of a second chance to pursue a thriving professional career.

But Poirier suffered a form of soccer impotence over the next couple of months that can doom a player whose reputation is defined by the number of goals he scores. By the time he was huffing heavily on that practice warm-up lap, Poirier still had scored just one goal for the year and his playing timing had severely diminished.

Back in April, Poirier, one of the best youth players to come out of the Washington, D.C. area, talked dreamily about living a soccer life full of pleasant professional moments.

"Playing pro soccer has been my dream since I was a little kid," he said then. "I'd like to play in MLS. If I have to be in division two or three for awhile, I'll do it."

That dream ultimately became another disappointment in a saga that began with so much hope and evolved into a comforting tale of maturity and acceptance.

Poirier, who grew up in Fairfax County, Virginia, showed potential early, making his first state and regional ODP team at age 13. Poirier played on Virginia ODP teams each year from ages 13 to 17 and Region I ODP teams from 13 to 16. At 16, he spent some time practicing with the U-20 National Team.

Poirier seems cloned to be a goal scorer. He's tall — 6' 2" — with a thin but muscular frame that supports 170 pounds. Good speed, a strong first step and an impressive sense of balance round out his prominent "striker" profile.

Royals midfielder Adam Wilson played with and against Poirier throughout his youth, and briefly with him in college.

"In high school, any ball Scott got inside the 18 was in the net," said Wilson. "He was a true forward. Scott was as big as a sophomore in high school as he is now. That's part of why he did so well. Now he's playing against men and he's not strong enough to hold people off the ball like he used to."

At Woodbridge High School, Poirier was a Gatorade High School Player of the Year in Virginia and was a Parade Magazine All-American.

He was equally impressive with top youth club teams in the Washington area. Pete England coached Poirier for three years on the VISTA Blackwatch, a youth club from Fairfax.

"I've never seen anyone as fast to the ball as him," said England.

England recalls a story that depicts the intensity and stubbornness that defined and ultimately helped diffuse a promising career. The U-17 Blackwatch were playing in the Tampa Sun Bowl tournament, one of the top youth tournaments in the country, against a team from St. Louis. In the first half, a St. Louis player ripped Poirier's shirt after Poirier had hit him in the groin. A card was given to the other player, but no card was given to Poirier.

Still, England knew Poirier was ready to burst. "As he walked to the sideline to get a new shirt, all he said was 'Don't take me out, I'm going to win this game,' " said England. "He goes back in and says a few words to

the referee. Within four minutes, he gets the ball atop the box, beats two players, dribbles past the goalie and puts us up 1-0. Then he drops back to play sweeper and sent the sweeper to play up front. He had never played sweeper before."

England's voice then rises with excitement. "I said, 'What are you doing?' He says, 'I've got it under control.' He was the best sweeper I've ever seen, knocked every ball out of our area and would not get beat."

Not all of England's memories of Poirier benefited his team. England kicked Poirier off the team twice. The first time occurred during a practice game in which England missed the first half and asked an assistant to run the team. When England showed up

With the Royals, Scott Poirier had trouble matching a stellar youth career.

at half time, he noticed his assistant sitting alone at the end of the bench.

"He says, 'Either he goes or I go,' " said England.

In England's words, Poirier told the coach to "fuck off, you're not running this team" from the field after the coach asked him to come out of the game. Poirier never played the second half. England told him to go home.

Poirier eventually apologized and returned to the team, but he lasted only a few more weeks.

"If you can put up with his horseshit, which nobody can, he can be in MLS," said England. "He's better than (D.C. United star) Jamie Moreno."

Still, college coaches wanted to give Poirier a chance. He was offered scholarships at William & Mary, Clemson and Seton Hall. He picked Seton

Hall, coached by Manny Schellscheidt, a former pro in Germany's first division who later played and coached in the North American Soccer League.

"Initially, there was no concern," said Schellscheidt, who first saw Poirier play when he coached a Region I ODP team of which Poirier was a member. "There were no problems on the regional team."

Poirier began the season as a freshman starter at forward. "He's a very gifted player in front of the goal," said Schellscheidt. "I've rarely seen someone who could finish chances the way Scott could."

Early in the season, Poirier starting having outbursts in games and practices from frustration. "Scoring was Scott's big forte," said Schellscheidt. "Some of his frustration came from him not scoring as frequently as he would like. If a scorer is not scoring, they don't do much else for the team. They don't play defense. You look at other solutions."

Soon, Poirier began games on the bench. His frustration grew and ultimately exploded during an away game on September 25, 1993 against Georgetown University. It was the first game in which Poirier appeared as a college player near his hometown.

Poirier scored in the first half but also earned an early yellow card for arguing with a referee. Later in the first half, Poirier received his second yellow card after committing a foul. His collegiate hometown debut turned disastrous; he was out of the game before half time.

And Poirier was not happy about the ejection. "He was upset and excited, steaming at the referee," said Schellscheidt. "Words were flying out his mouth on the way off the field. He was kind of out of control."

After the game—which Seton Hall won, 4-3, despite playing two men down toward the end—Poirier's mother asked Schellscheidt if she could take him home to Fairfax. Poirier never played again for Seton Hall.

Poirier, who portrays an easy-going and likable personality, has heard many versions of that story; he calmly downplayed the Seton Hall incident during a conversation two months into the Royals' 1998 season. "I've heard four or five different stories, from me spitting in his face to punching (Schellscheidt)," he said. "I never punched him. I never downgraded him. There was cursing, but it was not directed at him, like 'fuck you.' "

"I don't recall the words," said Schellscheidt, who spoke with compassion about Poirier. "Some of it could have been directed at me. I don't dwell too much on unpleasant situations. The sadness for me was to have him come (to Seton Hall) and not succeed. What this is all about is going to school, getting a degree and playing as well as you can."

Poirier's college career was not over. He played next at George Mason University. But his career there was brief as well.

George Mason Head Coach Gordon Bradley saw Poirier play "10 to 20 times" for Woodbridge High School and became a family friend. "He had the most potential of any player I've seen come out of high school in the Washington area," said Bradley. "He was a top class goal scorer. I like Scott. He's a quiet guy. You can sit down and have a nice talk with him, but his record on the field does not show that."

Poirier lasted barely a month at George Mason. Bradley recalls Poirier's time as a Patriot with slight discomfort. "During a practice, he said something derogatory to a coach," said Bradley. "And that was not the first time he said something like that. The players did not like him. He built his own nest, slept in it and he had to fly."

Poirier, who started playing soccer at age four, talks at times reluctantly—and frankly—about his past.

"I wasn't having fun playing soccer anymore," he says. "I was burned out. It was a combination of a lot of things. I was playing for 14 years. It got to be more business than pleasure. Was I pushed too hard? I wouldn't say my parents pushed me too hard.

"I guess I had a reputation as a kid as being hotheaded. At some point, you learn to control your emotions. It's good to have that passion and emotion, but you've got to learn to use it to your advantage. I've learned to control my temper now. That comes over time, just from growing up."

Poirier played no soccer for the next three years while he worked part-time as a computer consultant.

"I didn't miss it at first," said Poirier. "When I left, I was kind of sick of it. I didn't think I'd ever go back."

In January 1997, Bobby Lennon, a coach and owner of the Richmond Kickers when they won the USISL Premier Division and the U.S. Open Cup in 1995, called Poirier to play for his amateur team, the Virginia Kickers. Lennon set up the Kickers in 1996 as an apprenticeship program for players aged 18 to 23 who want to develop into professional players.

Kickers players pay Lennon $4,000 a year to be a part of the team. This fee covers all their team expenses except meals on trips. From August 1997 to May 1998 the team was based in Harrisonburg, Virginia before moving to Northern Virginia. Lennon liked Harrisonburg because of its proximity to James Madison University and its central location for travel throughout the East Coast. Also, the location provided the strong social environment he preferred for the players, who were required to attend college.

Members of the Kickers take college classes in the morning and practice in the afternoon. They stay together from mid-August to May. They play local amateur teams in the fall, train indoors and play games against youth national teams in Florida during the winter and compete against college teams and USISL teams in the spring. The Kickers, who play up to 80 games per year, also compete in the New York Hellenic Sport League, a highly competitive Greek amateur league in New York City.

Lennon asked Poirier to join the team, which he did in the fall of 1997. The previous winter he started playing indoor soccer at the Total Sports Pavilion in Woodbridge, Virginia. "It felt good," he says. "I was watching a little soccer on TV, with MLS and other games, and got interested again."

While playing some 40 games for the Kickers, Poirier attended Blue Ridge Community College, studying computer science.

The Kickers have helped develop some top talent. Josh Dunn, a defender who played in 14 games and scored 4 goals at the University of Virginia in 1995, started for the A-League's Hampton Roads Mariners during the 1998 season. Danny Britton was an all-D3 selection as a goalkeeper for the Roanoke Wrath during the 1998 season.

Poirier hoped that playing with the Kickers could help catapult him back to soccer superiority. "It was pretty good," said Poirier. "I just wanted to get to a tryout with a pro team and get out of there."

Lennon says Poirier joined the team with a lack of foresight. "Scott thought he could come out and it would just work for him like it did at the youth and high school level," said Lennon. "The layoff harmed him. He stepped right into the fire. He struggled. He was nonproductive. In the right environment, Scott would have a chance to do something. He needs to be around professionals full time. He's got to have a certain attitude and I don't think he knows what that attitude is.

"His best asset as a player is with his back to the goal. He could turn and shoot from anywhere in 30 yards and hit the back of the net. But his movement off the ball stifles his play. Any professional coach will want a forward that works hard."

But Lennon also saw a side of Poirier that was often absent during his youth. "Scott has a reputation as having a bad attitude," he said. "He didn't have the bad attitude with me. He just didn't have the right attitude. It wasn't anything that was his fault. He had so much success in the past, he didn't know what he was in for. He was close-minded. He didn't understand why things didn't work."

Still, in the spring of 1998, Poirier felt confident enough about his game to try professional soccer. He tried out unsuccessfully for the Charleston Battery of the A-League during spring break. "There were just too many players with more experience than me," he said.

The next stop was Myrtle Beach, home of the SeaDawgs, the 1997 D3 Atlantic Division champions. Poirier played one practice and a practice game with the team and was scheduled to play in another practice game that was rained out. He never heard from the coach again.

Lennon then suggested to Poirier that he try out for the Royals, which already had begun its preseason practices. "He made the Royals because of his reputation locally," said Lennon. "The Royals had nothing to lose. They weren't paying him anything."

Poirier joined the team at the end of March and soon signed a three-year contract. He felt comfortable with the fact that he knew a lot of the players from the Washington area that were on the team, and that his skills had returned enough to be a force with the Royals.

"I felt skill-wise I was up to par with the other players," he said. "I felt I had a good shot. A lot of people I played with at the regional level — Miles Joseph, Paul Grafer, Steve Jolley, Temoc Suarez — are playing MLS now. When I watch them, it makes me wonder what could have happened if I would have stayed. Not playing in college hurt me as far as playing pro. I think I could have made it in a second division (pro) team coming right out of college. But I try not to have regrets."

Gonzalo eagerly welcomed Poirier into the Royals camp. "This is the place where young players learn the game and develop into the game," he said in early April. "They deserve a chance. And I think Scott—he will play MLS someday."

B y the third game of the season, a home match in late April against the Delaware Wizards, Gonzalo started to experiment with Poirier at another position, placing the natural target forward at outside midfield. Barely 15 minutes into the match, Poirier was already breathing heavily. One time he walked past the Royals bench, clearly winded, and looked over as if to plead for a burst of oxygen or some sympathy from his teammates. It became painfully obvious that Poirier did not possess a prolific work rate or much endurance, a requirement for an effective outside midfielder.

Poirier was moved up front after Rachid Mahboub, his replacement at forward, received a red card in the 17th minute. But Poirier seemed too gassed to be effective even as a target. He was subbed out in the 41st minute.

Poirier's apparent lack of fitness persuaded Gonzalo to sit him at the start of the fourth game of the season, an away match against the Reading Rage. Poirier came in late in the 4-1 loss to the Rage, after the game had already been decided, and was a late substitute in the next game at home against the Rhode Island Stingrays.

Gonzalo did not select Poirier for the team's disastrous road trip to New England, where they lost three U.S. Open Cup games in three days and several key players suffered serious injury.

"It was simply a numbers game," he said. "I could take 17 players. I had more faith in Rachid than Scott."

Tension understandably permeated the following week at practice. Gonzalo gathered the Virginia State team he would coach at the regional amateur tournament the following weekend to practice with the Royals.

Gonzalo showed his growing displeasure with Poirier during a full-field practice game pitting the Royals against the State team. Some 15 minutes into the game, Poirier reacted lazily after hitting a pass that was intercepted by an opponent. Gonzalo, already testy due to the team's recent poor play, did not react well. What frustrated Gonzalo the most about his team's play during the losing streak was their inability to apply defensive pressure at midfield, especially after losing possession. Poirier had just committed that kind of error. Gonzalo quickly yelled to Poirier to leave the field.

Watching Poirier walk off the field, I waited to see if he would erupt into a flurry of verbal outrage. His expression read bewilderment, his walk bore purpose. He initially walked off the field away from Gonzalo.

But Poirier's curiosity ultimately grew too strong. Within moments, he calmly confronted Gonzalo.

"What's that about?"

Gonzalo stared at the field.

"You're not working hard. You missed practice last week."

"What do you mean? I missed two practices in 30 days. I can't score a goal if I'm in for 15 minutes. I scored a goal in the first game. It takes a while."

Gonzalo did not respond, instead watching the game more intensely, his hand on his knees in a half crouched position, signaling his indifference to Poirier's plea.

Following a moment of silence, Poirier admirably walked away, waiting until he was far enough from Gonzalo so the coach could barely hear his muttered response.

"That's fuckin' bullshit," he said.

Did Gonzalo treat Poirier fairly? Gonzalo's claim that Poirier was missing practice was unfounded. All players missed practice regularly, due to job commitments, and Poirier had just recently started a job as a technical recruiter. Up to that point, Poirier actually was one of the players who attended practice most often. But he was not the hardest worker on the field. In a sense, he was a tailor-made target forward, aggressive to the ball in his space and possessing a knack for unloading well-paced shots on goal.

But Gonzalo wanted Poirier to do more — to mark defenders and pressure the opponent into mistakes. It seemed a case of a coach's desire not matching a player's preferred role.

A couple of days later, Gonzalo explained his concerns about Poirier's play more specifically.

"He has great potential, but he has to be more aggressive," he said. "He has not shown it the last couple of weeks. If he does what I tell him to, he will be one of the best players on the team."

Poirier did not receive much of a chance to do what the coach wanted him to do after that practice. He dressed for the team's next home game, but did not play. Poirier was not on the initial roster for the next road trip —two games on successive days in late May against the South Carolina Shamrocks and the Charlotte Eagles. But he was called in late for the Charlotte game after Royals defender Steve Gill returned home early due to a family illness. Poirier played the final 15 minutes of that game.

Poirier started his new job as a technical recruiter two days before the trip to the Carolinas. He was chagrined about how he was treated on the trip.

"They called me at 9:30 in the morning to meet a couple hours later for the ride to South Carolina," said Poirier. "I couldn't leave then but joined them in time for the next game. I drove six hours by myself. And then I only play 15 minutes against Charlotte. They said they'd pay me gas money. I paid for my own hotel room. I was never reimbursed."

The Eagles game was the last time Poirier played a game in a Royals uniform. He dressed for the final time two games later at home against the Roanoke Wrath in mid June. Poirier's presence at practice then became more random. He did not show up for days in succession. His interest seemed to wane.

"When I started the job, I was brought on board because they had a backlog," he said. "I was working late hours, was out of town half the week."

During a night home match against the Wilmington Hammerheads on July 8, Poirier sat in the sparse bleachers, huddled closely with his girlfriend and surrounded by a couple of injured Royals players. He was a mere 50 yards behind the bench, but he seemed miles away from the team he once hoped would revive his career. And, unknown to Poirier, his fate had already been decided.

Minutes before the Wilmington game, I asked Royals General Manager Sherif Shehata to comment on Poirier's future with the team. He stood calmly near the stadium press box, some 15 rows behind where Poirier sat.

"He's been cut," Shehata said calmly with a trace of compassion and a bit of remorse. "We like Scott, but he just wasn't able to make the commitment. We'll probably tell him next week."

Gonzalo's chat with Poirier that night was equally ominous.

"I told him since he didn't show up for practice, I'm thinking of releasing him," he said. "He didn't really say something back. He's not going to (improve) because of his attitude, the way he trains. He's very lazy. He doesn't allow you to push him."

Poirier had trouble understanding why he lost his standing with the Royals. "When I wasn't working and first started playing with them, I was going to practice all the time," he said. "One day I was in the starting lineup. I was asking the coach what was wrong. He said, 'You're doing fine, you're doing great.' It was very difficult and very frustrating."

Two weeks after the Wilmington game, when I called Poirier to ask how soccer was going for him, he seemed unaware he was cut (he said in November that he was never told he was released from the team). I did not want to tell him that I was told he would be cut, so I did not mention it. I felt he should hear the news from management. Poirier apparently had settled into his new job, which he started in mid-May.

"I noticed you haven't come out to practice much lately. Is work more of a priority now than soccer?"

"Yeah, soccer does not pay the bills. Work is definitely a priority now. I think I'm going on a trip to Raleigh next week."

"For work?"

"Yeah."

"Have your goals regarding soccer changed?"

"Is this for the book?"

"Yeah."

"I'd rather not talk about that now, if you don't mind. Is that okay?"

"Sure. It's up to you. I'd just like to put in perspective what's happening with your soccer."

"Maybe some other time."

"All right. Maybe we'll see you at practice."

I never did.

When contacted at home in mid-November, Poirier was not thinking much about soccer. He thought more about his job and personal security. He had just moved into a rental house and talked about buying a house of his own soon.

In late July, soon after he stopped playing for the Royals, Poirier called Bobby Lennon to ask him if he needed coaching help with the Virginia Kickers. But Poirier could not adjust his work schedule to attend the team's 2 p.m. practices. He's considered coaching youth teams in the Northern Virginia area. He said he thinks infrequently about playing again.

"When I called Bobby, that's really the last time I thought about anything to do with soccer," he said. "I really haven't put too much thought into it since then."

REBORN IN ROANOKE

I f the Northern Virginia Royals players composed one phrase that would reflect the struggles of their rookie season in the USISL, it probably would be "A Road to Nowhere." About two-thirds through the season, the Royals claimed just one victory in seven away matches. And with seven games remaining in their 22-game season, and only one at home, the Royals were scratching and clawing up the rickety playoff fence. As they departed for Roanoke, Virginia in mid-July, they stood five points behind Wilmington for the sixth and final playoff spot.

True to form, the road for the Royals would again be rough.

They held an optional practice the day after the gratifying win over Wilmington, leaving some players with two days off before departing for the Saturday evening match against Roanoke. About one dozen players showed up for some light stretching and a 6 v 6 game that took up about a third of the field and lasted about an hour and a half.

The win over Wilmington ended a four-game losing streak. Not surprisingly, the players had not been so relaxed in practice in more than a month.

The small-sided game was played to 31 points. A goal between two cones placed about two yards apart counted as one point and was four points when it was "megged" (kicked through a player's legs) in goal. A meg that did not lead to a score yielded one point as well. If the ball entered the goal off the ground, it was disallowed.

While the players joked and jived on the field, Silvino Gonzalo mostly sat alone and peacefully off to the side on a set of small aluminum bleachers, letting his players enjoy a day away from his commands and guidance.

It was a perfect setting for Mark Vita to show traces of his outgoing personality. After his opposing team disallowed a goal that they said was not on the ground as it went through the cones, he responded in typical juvenile fashion.

"All right, we can play like that," he said, walking briskly towards his goal. He then stood in front of his team's goal as an attack approached. Vita at the last second lay face down on the ground in front of the goal, his body stretching the length of the cones.

Not all was jovial with the Royals, though. One no-show at practice was Steve Gill, who walked off the Royals home field in a huff toward the end of the Wilmington game.

It was an uncharacteristic exchange between a player and coach who had formed a strong friendship. Gill started playing for Gonzalo in 1993 with Iberia. As a gritty sweeper and vocal team leader, Gill helped Gonzalo and Iberia win the national amateur title in 1996.

Gill, 29, from Newcastle, England, learned the game "as soon as he could stand up," he said. As a youth, he played often at a practice field about 100 yards behind his house. He started training with Newcastle's school boy program when he was 13, the same program that developed England's National Team star Paul Gascoigne, one of the most feared and volatile midfielders in England in the 1990s.

Gill learned how to win at a young age. He won a national championship in 1985 with Willington High School. His club team, the Northumberland Boys, won a national championship in 1986.

Gill parlayed his soccer success into a four-year scholarship at James Madison University in Harrisonburg, Virginia. At Madison, he earned All-Conference honors and All-South Atlantic honors three times.

He then went home to England and played for Tow Law F.C. in the semi-pro English Northern League. Gill returned to the U.S. in 1993 for work and started playing immediately with Iberia.

In 1996, Gill was offered a contract to play for the Richmond Kickers but declined because he was not comfortable with the offer. At the same time, he received a job offer from Xerox and had just met his future wife, Wendi. He opted to stay in the Washington, D.C. area, where he works as a sales manager for Xerox.

Gill hopes to play soccer at the D3 level until his mid-30s. But if he continues to have periodic spats with Gonzalo, his career could be cut short. Gill played D3 because of Gonzalo and has no desire to play for any other team.

"Maybe I'll even go into coaching the Royals when my playing days are over. But I'll probably have to curtail my temper a little bit," he said laughing. "As long as I keep it on the field, I think I'm doing all right."

A short temper forced gritty central defender Steve Gill off the pitch for a couple of games.

Gill's outburst as he walked off the field at the end of the Hammerheads game in early July was not the first time his temper flared as a Royal. To the surprise and chagrin of some players, Gonzalo asked his team to run a series of hard sprints at the end of the first practice following the Royals' trip to New England, in which they played three games in three days. The practice on May 19 took place two days after the third game of the trip and the players were still clearly fatigued.

The sprints were set up in three sets: from the end line to the 18-yard line twice; from the end line to mid-field twice; and finally, from one end line to the other end line once.

After the set to mid-field, Gill's loud grumbles clearly reflected his displeasure. Most of the other players felt the same way, and they mumbled and groaned under their breath. But Gill had the balls to speak his mind.

Assistant coach Matt Badiee would have none of it.

"Sit out! Get out of here!," Badiee ordered Gill.

"I might sit out Sunday, too," said Gill loudly, referring to the Royals' next game against Eastern Shore five days later.

John Pascarella, huffing heavily and bent over slightly with his hands on his knees, found the moment appropriate for some self-deprecation. He made an offhand reference to his penchant for random bickering.

"See what I've started?" he said, with a smirk of disgust. "I'm such an asshole." Pascarella's comment provided a brief distraction from the tense moment.

Nearly two months later, as the team gathered for the trip to Roanoke, Gill arrived in a hotel parking lot in Tysons Corner wondering if Gonzalo would take him on the trip. They talked quietly and civilly for a few minutes. Gill then drove away without saying a word to anyone else.

"He said he wanted to take me but that Mo Sheta and Sherif said it's best if he not take me," said Gill. "At that time I understood what I had done was stupid."

Gill also missed a road trip the next weekend to Myrtle Beach. "I didn't want to go to Myrtle Beach," he said. "I just didn't feel it was time to come back. Part of my thinking was, I was still suspended." Gill returned to practice after the Myrtle Beach weekend.

Gonzalo explained his decision while sitting in the lobby of a Best Western Hotel in Roanoke as his players stirred about and checked in the day of the Wrath game.

"Steve asked me, 'You don't think I can control myself?'" said Gonzalo. "I said, 'No.' Steve is a good man, but it was very disgraceful what he did. He showed he does not respect the bench. He's not helping the team or the owners. I feel bad because I like Steve. He should be a leader, like Ricky (Engelfried)."

Without Gill in the lineup against Roanoke, Engelfried—the team's true utility player—filled in at sweeper. Jeff Standish, a steady and sturdy central defender, replaced Engelfried at stopper.

In the Wrath, the Royals faced a team that had progressed much better than they had since the first time they met in mid June. The Wrath endured a heavy stretch of games, winning three of five matches in 22 days, and were in third place with 21 points. One of those wins was a 7-0 trouncing over the Eastern Shore Sharks, whom the Royals barely beat, 3-2. The

Royals, in seventh place, had played just twice since they lost to the Wrath on June 13 (one game was rained out), winning one and losing one.

The two teams were also heading in a different direction off the field. While no Royals players were paid, about a half-dozen or so Wrath players earned from $200 to $500 per month. The Wrath also provided complimentary rent and utilities for nine players in two houses, and work at its summer soccer camps.

Several players worked full time, including team captain and part owner Grayson Prillaman, an All-American at Roanoke College in the early 1990s. Prillaman, a stock broker, played for the Washington Mustangs in the mid 1990s.

The Wrath played their home matches at Victory Stadium, an old cement facility owned by the Roanoke City Park and Recreation Department. The stadium seats around 12,000 but the Wrath had been averaging only about 500 a game.

General Manager and Head Coach Bob Bigney joined the team on March 31. "I was kind of hoping all our sponsors were already on board," he said with a laugh while standing in the middle of their narrow home field about an hour before game time.

The Wrath snatched seven major sponsors, including a local auto parts dealer, U.S. Cellular phone company and Budweiser beer. They also bartered commercial time on a local cable television station.

Still, the Wrath endured some hardship their first season. New sod was placed in the stadium in March so the Wrath could enjoy a comfortable pitch for their first home game on April 18. But an appearance by the popular Dave Matthews Band attracted 30,000 fans during heavy rain. The event ruined much of the field before the Wrath could enjoy it. They were forced to play their first five games at a different facility while the field was repaired with new sod.

Three months later, the field still showed signs of repair. One-inch strips of dirt stretched throughout small portions of the field at the seams where lateral rows of sod were joined.

Gonzalo was more concerned with the field's lack of width. In his pregame speech, he urged his players to mark the Wrath players closely. The Royals failed to do so on a Wrath corner kick just 90 seconds into the game.

Prillaman tapped in a free ball in front of the goal mouth to put the Wrath up 1-0.

Pascarella put together another strong performance in the first half. He thwarted a one-on-one chance with a kick save while falling backwards. With four minutes remaining, he kept the Royals down by one at the half by diving to his left to deflect a hard shot just wide of the right post.

Gonzalo pitched no fit during his half time chat. He simply encouraged patience and said that the Royals were playing well. "We're getting them," he said. He did, however, shuffle his lineup a bit, moving Mark Vita up front and Tim Prisco back more into the middle.

Gonzalo was radiating with confidence when he walked up to me as I stood behind the bench just before the start of the second half. "We are going to win this game," he said, with a wink.

It took the Royals 27 minutes to tie the game. Matt Ferry kicked in a loose ball after Wrath goalkeeper Danny Britton deflected a curling cross by Vita. Two subsequent solid chances by the Wrath could have hammered the first nail in the Royals' coffin. A soft Roanoke shot glanced off the cross bar in the 82nd minute and Pascarella continued his masterful effort when he tapped a hard header over the cross bar in the 88th minute.

The game almost ended in overtime and 19-year-old Maxx Henry-Frazier could have been the hero. With just more than three minutes remaining in the 15-minute overtime, Henry-Frazier found himself standing about 10 yards beyond his near post with the ball at his feet and no field defender near him. His shot was on goal but Britton, an All-League selection for 1998, dove quickly and brilliantly to his right and at the last moment slapped the ball harmlessly beyond the post.

Henry-Frazier's missed opportunity was the best chance for either team to score in overtime. For the first and only time all season, the Royals were heading to a shoot-out.

In the shoot-out, the player starts from 35 yards out and has five seconds to shoot the ball. The only defender is the goalkeeper. Each team has five chances to score before entering a sudden-death situation. If the teams are tied after five attempts, each team is given one chance to score until a team has gained an advantage.

The Royals had worked on the shoot-out only twice in practice and it showed in the first three rounds. Rachid Mahboub, Jeff Standish and Adam Vigon failed to score while Roanoke converted two of its first three chances.

If the Royals missed any more attempts, they would return home with a fifth loss in their last six games and, perhaps more importantly, deflated spirits. But the Royals showed pure moxie in the last two rounds, aided in part by some veteran gamesmanship and solid execution by Pascarella.

In the fourth round, Tim Prisco scored for the Royals while Pascarella made a dramatic kick save of the Wrath's ensuing attempt by defender Mike Botta. The Royals still could not afford another miss. Next up was Adam Wilson, Gonzalo's much-maligned midfielder. Wilson calmly hit a hard shot past the keeper, forcing the Wrath to convert their final attempt to avoid sudden death in the shoot-out.

Pascarella then played a little mind game with Prillaman. Just before the midfielder approached the ball, the 31-year-old keeper walked off the goal line to confer with the referee for about 30 seconds. Pascarella was trying to freeze the shooter, who looked a little confused and seemed distracted. It worked. Prillaman's shot never made it on goal as Pascarella stopped it with another kick save.

In the sixth round, Matt Ferry missed for the Royals, shooting left as the goalkeeper saved it with a kick. Wrath defender Chris Segaar then blasted his shot over the cross bar.

Alberto Ogando stepped up next for the Royals with a little insight. "As I was watching the keeper I noticed that he dived every time to his left," said Ogando. Using the outside of his right foot, Ogando hit a hard, low shot that slid by on the keeper's right as he dove left. Pascarella then came up big again, stopping forward Andy Smith's final attempt with his chest as he dove right.

Considering what they had just accomplished, the Royals responded surprisingly with contained glee. Their celebration was quick and seemed rather dispassionate. But there were subtle signs of joy.

"We're gonna have some beers now," said Ferry as he walked, smiling, towards the locker room. For the first time on a road trip—some three months into the season—the Royals had permission to drink beer after a game. Ah, the simple rewards of victory.

Gonzalo commented briefly after the game as he walked proudly through the locker room. "Guys, thank you," he said. "That's a big win."

It could have been bigger. If they had taken a regulation win, the Royals would have earned three points instead of the one point awarded for a shoot-out victory. The win placed them five points behind the sixth place Wilmington Hammerheads.

The players seemed oblivious to their playoff predicament. Outside the locker room, Pascarella stood in the gravelly parking lot as the lingering lights of the stadium shone Royally behind him, casting him in a hero's shadow. His proud and smiling wife stood by his side.

In a sense, Pascarella was an unlikely hero. Some Royals players and coaches thought he might not have lasted so long into the season. After the home opener, in which Pascarella visibly showed his displeasure with not starting, his priorities changed dramatically.

"Not playing was disappointing," Pascarella said while reflecting on the season in November. "My commitment to the team changed very early. The turning point really happened at the opening game. Up until that point, my priorities were my soccer, my family and my work. Soccer came at the bottom after that first game. If I could have jumped ship for a better team, I would have and my priorities would have been soccer at the top again. Maybe I went into it with my expectations too high."

Pascarella satisfied many expectations with his stellar effort during the shoot-out. Outside the locker room, he explained his crafty maneuvering during the fifth round of the shoot-out. "I tried to waste as much time as I could," he said. "I asked the referee, How many more shots were left? Was it the last round? What was the score? I used to fake a cramp to delay the game, but you can't do that in a shoot-out."

By midnight, Gonzalo and the rest of the coaching staff were mingling with many of the Royals players at Cabbage & Corn, a trendy night spot in downtown Roanoke. The airy club featured many choices of micro-brewed beer from two bars, a small, overcrowded dance floor, a brick oven in the back for pizza, and an outdoor deck on the second floor.

The Royals did most of their socializing as a team during road trips. A few players—mostly Ogando, Pascarella, Vigon, Thiombiano, and Kerns—regularly joined Gonzalo and Badiee for a relaxing cup of coffee or other similar beverage after practice. The younger players—Vita, Prisco, Kuykendall and the rarely-rostered Garth Campbell—occasionally socialized together at area night clubs. Sometimes a few players ventured for a couple refreshing post-game beverages at P.J. Skidoos, a restaurant located across the street from their home field in Fairfax, Virginia. But for the most part, while at home, they were a disjointed social group.

That is not surprising for a professional team. Some players are married and spend more time at home than out with the guys. Most players worked full-time. That made it difficult to socialize frequently after practice as a team.

But a strong sense of social unity prevailed within the team at Cabbage & Corn after the Roanoke game. Many Royals players and coaches consumed several beers. Several acquired a jolly drunken state. There were more smiles and laughs in the next two hours than on all the previous road trips combined. Gonzalo's charm and sense of humor was rampant. The normally reserved Engelfried, made more lucid by the alcohol, opined excitedly at length about many facets of soccer and aspects of life. Mahboub, Vita and Kuykendall worked the rooms comfortably, dancing and chatting the night away with a bevy of strangers. The uninhibited merriment was good to see. It was the only time all season the Royals won successive games.

Once Cabbage & Corn closed, a few players ventured to an after-hours dance club a few blocks away. An after-hours dance club in Roanoke? It proved to be less impressive than it sounded. Only a few patrons mingled inside, so all but two players headed back to the hotel. It was nearing 3 a.m.

Curfew? No such thing.

CAN'T MAKE THE CLUB IN THE TUB

Numerous injuries marred and almost defined my collegiate athletic career. I sprained my right ankle eight times, most often during my last two seasons. An ankle sprain is a strange injury for a middle-distance runner; usually, pulled muscles are more prevalent. But the bony structure of my ankles made them susceptible to severe twists and turns.

Most sprains happened while cross-country training on a golf course. One happened while I was playing in a touch football game on astroturf, an offense that resulted in a severe verbal lashing from my coach. A team rule forbade us from playing any contact sports. Embarrassingly, street curbs were also a culprit a couple of times.

The most severe injury—an Achilles tendon strain—happened even before I attended my first class at the University of Maryland.

While injured, it seemed that I spent more time rehabilitating in a training room than I spent in the library. Actually, I probably spent more time in a car than in the library. And I didn't have a car while in college.

A training room can be a depressing place. Rarely is an injured athlete in a good mood once they walk in the room. Your teammates are improving their skills and physical conditioning while your fitness and skill level gradually fade.

Injured athletes know they're missing valuable practice time and could lose a position on the team, or more drastically, be cut from the team and lose their scholarship. And despite the appreciated efforts of the trainers to cheer you up, most athletes moan, complain or sleep during their treatment.

The training room I frequented was set up for soccer, track and field, lacrosse and baseball athletes and was the smallest of the three training rooms at the school. Our training room was not a place one ventured for an emotional boost. Red and white tile floors, red wooden taping tables and pipes running the length of the ceilings mirrored images of a waiting room in an old hospital.

The palatial training room at Maryland was in the football building. Twice the size of our training room, it featured cushioned tables, larger

whirlpools, music blaring from speakers in the ceiling and even a bathroom.

Although more comforting, I did not yearn for treatment there. Receiving treatment in the football building usually meant the physician for the school's athletic teams needed to see you. After my Achilles tendon injury had not improved much in two months, I was sent over to see an

A history of ankle injuries forced the author to take preventive measures before each practice .

orthopedist at the football training room. He placed me in a cast for one month to completely immobilize the ankle joint and enhance the healing of the tendon.

My first semester in college was turning into a disaster. Missing a fall season of training can have a severe impact on a runner's performance during the indoor and outdoor seasons. Hobbling around in a cast did not ease my anxiety about the impending competitive season.

There are, however, some comforting elements of a training room. The whirlpool, with it's swirling, warm water, soothed the aches and pains of a lingering injury. The comforting touch of an athletic trainer sometimes helped to make the mind wander from the inconvenience of physical injury and the arduous process of recovery.

With good intentions, the trainers at Maryland erected signs on the walls to help motivate the injured athletes. The most impressive was the "Pyramid of Success" by former basketball coach and legend John Wooden. The pyramid, displayed on about a four-square-foot board, promoted about one dozen elements that would help create a successful athlete, including determination, perseverance, discipline and teamwork.

I did find disturbing one sign that hung annoyingly on a wall close to the whirlpool. It served as a compelling reminder of the realities of athletics. It read: "You Can't Make the Club in the Tub."

It didn't take an ignorant college student-athlete to figure that out.

My first physical complication with the Royals occurred a mere three weeks after I started practicing. And it happened off the field, the morning after an invigorating practice session.

It was barely 8 a.m. and I was eating breakfast. A story in the morning newspaper piqued my interest and I leaned forward to more easily read it. I put my elbows on the table and the movement triggered a dull pain in the left side of my neck that increased dramatically when I rose later to walk upstairs to my office. Within 30 minutes, the pain circled my neck and stopped on the right side. A quick turn of the head prompted sharp piercing pains, as if someone was hammering 10-penny nails in my neck.

I quickly set up an appointment to see my chiropractor, Dr. Scott Muzinski. I have been visiting Dr. Muzinski once a week for several years. Under normal fitness circumstances, a weekly visit usually kept my skeletal structure in check and my muscles in balance. But I had increased the stress on my body while training with the Royals.

According to Dr. Muzinski, I had pinched a nerve in my neck. A pinched nerve, he explained, usually happens when the ligament or cartilage attached to a bone, or a muscle attached to a tendon, presses on a nerve. "It's like when you have a garden hose filled with water and you step on the hose and cut off the water," he said. "That pinching causes the pain." It's difficult to think that putting my elbows on the table could cause a pinched nerve. But that motion actually triggered an injury that may have occurred as far back as a few days before I felt the pain.

If there was any consolation, the timing was good. We had a day off from practice that day. I took advantage of the downtime and visited my sports massage therapist. The one-hour session reaped multiple muscular benefits. I returned to practice the following day with a stiff neck, but not too impaired to play.

I was waiting for my body to react like this. It had been feeling too good for too long. For about the next six weeks, I stayed relatively pain free. Still, I had a couple of bad days, like the one on June 9.

That day I felt awful, the worst of any practice all season. During a brief fitness workout, which involved running pickups from one corner of the midfield line to the far corner of the end line, I could not even keep up with 46-year-old John Ormassa, the team manager who trained with us on occasion. A swift pace was not Ormassa's hallmark.

As hard as I tried to push, my muscles just would not respond. On the first sprint, I felt tightness in my lower back, so I backed off and finished the rest of the workout running at about 70 percent.

I stood around during the rest of practice and let a light, soothing rain pelt me. The rain revived me a bit. Perhaps it was trying to knock some sense into me. Maybe I should be doing what most 40-year-olds were doing at that moment—having a cocktail to unwind from a work day, tossing a wee one in the air or helping to plot their child's path through the educational maze.

The rain would have had to be a torrential downpour for me to continue those thoughts much longer. Still, it felt good to be out there. I wondered how many guys would have wished they were exactly right where I was—in the middle of an invigorating soccer practice, pursuing a dream of playing pro ball.

The big one hit about one month later. The reason my normally weak ankles had endured practicing three or four times a week so well was due primarily to the soft ground. But once the rains stopped and the fields started to parch around early June, the toll on my body increased. I should have seen it coming. The smart move would have been to start preventive therapy to strengthen my ankles and surrounding muscles before the pain set in. But sometimes when you feel good, you get a foolish sense that nothing can go wrong.

I felt lazy on July 13 and spent less time than usual before practice stretching my calves and Achilles tendons. We finished the practice with a 30-minute game. I tried to play harder than the rest of the team. It was crunch time for me. Gonzalo had to make a decision soon if I was to make my professional debut. Only five games remained on the schedule and two would be against teams battling the Royals for the last playoff spot.

Starting in early July, I tried to gauge Gonzalo's interest in letting me suit up for a match. At that time, Gonzalo faced a dilemma. The team was struggling to make the playoffs, but he said he would try to figure out a way to get me in a game. I stressed to Gonzalo that I did not want my playing time to hinder the team's run at post-season play. He assured me everything would be okay. Still, I was skeptical.

I figured the best way to convince Gonzalo that I should play was to work hard in practice. So I approached the scrimmage during July 13 as a big game. My spring amateur season in the NVSL had been over for about one month and Gonzalo, wisely, rarely set up scrimmages in practice once he was halfway through the season. After playing 17 games, practices were a good time for the Royals to physically recover, refine skills and technique and stay tactically sharp. But I was itching to play in a game situation.

I was normally one of the last ones called in during practice games. But the training on July 13 took place two days after the Royals' big shootout win in Roanoke and was the first practice since the game. About a half dozen players opted out of practice. With fewer players to choose from, Gonzalo placed me at left flank to start the game.

Both Achilles tendons felt tight as the game began, but I soon ignored the discomfort, aided by adrenaline and the motivation to show Gonzalo I was ready to suit up. I walked off the field content that I had put forth a solid effort and confident that I had made Gonzalo's decision to play me even tougher.

But about an hour after walking off the field, the first steps out of my car after the ride home brought excruciating pain. I nearly fell over after taking two steps. Both Achilles tendons had swelled up to the point of near immobility.

A month-long ordeal tolerating continuous pain and extensive therapy was about to begin. I felt compelled to the point of obsession to work through the challenge.

Before my Achilles tendons nearly collapsed on July 13, the extent of my therapy was about 10 minutes of ice massage on the sore areas after practice. But after July 13, my therapy routine changed dramatically. Each night after practice, I added manual massage to the ice treatments. If I missed an ice session, the tendons would be so stiff I would need a cane to get out of bed the next morning.

The next day, I missed my first practice of the season due to the injury. All I could do at the team's next practice on Wednesday was watch. I hoped that by the following Monday, I would be back on the pitch. The Royals had the day off on Thursday to rest for a crucial two-games-in-two-days road trip to Myrtle Beach starting on Friday.

When I joined them for their next practice on Monday, it was clear that my resolve to play a game for the Royals was about to face its stiffest challenge. Slow jogging felt the worst of any activity, for two reasons: It was done as a warm-up at the beginning of practice when muscles were the tightest and the poor dynamic quality of a slow jog did not help take one's mind off the physical discomfort. When involved in an up-tempo drill or game, it was easier for my thoughts to wander away from the pain.

By this part of the season, most of the players suffered some nagging injury, from a deep muscle bruise to a lingering hamstring strain. I did not expect much sympathy from the team, and I did not seek it. Rather, I tried to limit movements that aggravated the injury. I tried to run about half-way up on my toes. Extending my heels caused great discomfort. Sharp cutting or turning also aggravated the injured areas. So I tempered the severe movements and tried to move forward and backward as much as possible. Lateral movement, so crucial in soccer, was made very difficult.

I tried to take advantage of things I could control, the most obvious being fitness maintenance. On the days the team did not practice or when they had a game, I spent as much time as possible in a pool—running or swimming—or on a stationary recumbent bicycle.

The workouts were designed to maintain the relative speed and power I had developed in three months of training. I simulated interval workouts on the recumbent bicycle with a 10 or 15 minute warm-up followed by 15 minutes of one-minute hard, one-minute easy. I increased strength training for my legs with low-repetition, heavy-weighted and quick exercises to simulate explosive motion. I tried to keep sharp the fast twitch fibers in my muscles.

Working out in the pool became a nice reprieve from the tedium of training during the hottest part of the summer. Refreshing water rushing over my muscles as I worked out cooled off the body quickly. This allowed me to work even harder without feeling dehydrated or overly fatigued.

In the meantime, I began a three-time-a-week therapy routine that involved electric stimulation, ultrasound and manual massage on the injured areas. Staying fit to play soccer was becoming a second part-time job.

It soon became obvious that for the last month of the season, I had to adapt to an unnatural method of training for and playing soccer. While the Royals fought as a team to make the playoffs, I fought to keep alive my chance to wear just one time the Royals' blue and gold.

15
CHASING THE CHIHUAHUAS

Whatever momentum the Royals had developed following their win at Roanoke was diminished by the end of the next weekend. They lost two games on the road in mid-July, this time to the Myrtle Beach SeaDawgs. The second game was played as a make-up for a home match that was rained out in late June.

Does economics rule the league? The Royals were fighting for their playoff lives. Rather than make the situation as comfortable as possible for the players and reschedule the rained out game at home with at least one recovery day between matches, the teams agreed to play both contests in two days at Myrtle Beach, a team that was fighting for the Atlantic division title with an 11-6 record.

The Royals lost 3-1 on Friday night but stormed back the next night in what Gonzalo called "a great game" played by his team. On Saturday, the Royals led 2-0 after 55 minutes. But the game was tied at the 70th minute. The Royals took a 3-2 lead on a penalty kick by Mark Vita after Leonardo Thiombiano was taken down in the box. The SeaDawgs then scored off a corner kick with five minutes remaining and tied the game. A minute and a half later, SeaDawgs midfielder Jeff Johnson, who already had three assists in the match, converted from 40 yards out, the ball rocketing devastatingly (for the Royals) just inside the upper left corner of the goal.

Despite the Royals giving up four goals in the last 35 minutes, Gonzalo felt good about his team.

"I can almost say the team is playing the best soccer in the league right now," he said a couple days after the game.

But his non-D.C. United goalkeepers caused him great concern.

"We don't have good goalkeepers," he said. "The team does not play with confidence with the goalkeepers we have."

When the Royals played next—their last home game of the season the following weekend against the Charlotte Eagles—one of Gonzalo's most cherished defenders would not be on the pitch.

During the weekend of the Charlotte game, Chris Jones was in Phoenix, Arizona working at the 1998 U. S. Youth Soccer Association (USYSA) National Championships, an annual event that decides national titles in the U-16 to U-20 age groups for boys and girls. Adidas is a major sponsor of USYSA.

Jones had not played for the Royals since June 13 because of work. For about six weeks, he traveled the country plying his trade as an adidas marketing representative.

I also attended the tournament, covering the event for U.S. Youth Soccer, one of my publishing company's clients. During most of the whirlwind four days in Phoenix, the Royals were far from our minds. But when Saturday evening arrived, I anxiously awaited the result of the match.

A win against Charlotte would ease the Royals' end-of-season stretch—three away games during the next two weekends. The Royals stood five points behind Wilmington, which held the last playoff spot in the Atlantic Division in sixth place. Wilmington and the Royals were scheduled to play each other the last game of the season.

Beating Charlotte would be no easy task. They were the 1997 D3 runners-up, boasted a 9-4 record and stood playoff-secure in third place in the Atlantic Division.

I discovered the game's result at about 10 p.m. Phoenix time and quickly searched for Jones to provide an update. I spotted him sitting in a set of bleachers reading a magazine inside the comfortably air-conditioned adidas promotional tent.

"Jonesy, I've got a Royals result," I said.

"I don't think I wanna know," he said, not looking up from his magazine. His indifference came from sensing the worst and remembering how they had lost the weekend before. In the previously mentioned and ominous words of Adam Vigon, "Fuckin' ay, this is the Royals." Jones had every right to be cautious.

Silvino Gonzalo had proven himself to be a clever orator during his pre-game speeches. Before the Charlotte game, he used a couple new twists—animal and super-hero metaphors.

"Possession of the ball is vital," he said in a calm locker room. "Make them chase it. You must run like chihuahuas."

He later encouraged Mark Vita to be "busy."

"You've been playing great," he said to Vita. "Run everywhere. You're the six-million-dollar man."

Vita proved himself worthy of his moniker when he scored the first Royals goal and tied the game in the 20th minute after Charlotte had scored one minute before.

Charlotte scored 10 minutes later following a disputed no-call on an apparent off side. That no-call ultimately helped transform the potentially incendiary Pascarella into a firestorm. A few minutes after the no-call, Pascarella ran from his goal area toward an assistant referee screaming and waving his arms, to complain about what he thought were missed off-side calls. The referee stopped Pascarella and said, "I understand your frustration," before pointing him back toward his goal.

At the 44-minute mark, Charlotte was called for off side. The call met Pascarella's approval. He held his hands over his head and clapped sarcastically, prompting many in the crowd of around 200 to join in.

The fans had plenty to clap about after the Royals took the lead, 3-2, in the 74th minute following goals by Alberto Ogando and Mark Vita.

But, again, the Royals could not hold on. Charlotte converted a free kick with six minutes remaining in regulation, forcing the Royals into their fourth overtime match of the season. Four minutes into the sudden-death overtime, the Eagles stole the game from the Royals on a freaky goal. A Charlotte throw-in floated dangerously towards the goal area. Pascarella jumped to punch the ball clear, but he collided with a Charlotte player attempting to head it in goal. The ball squirted away from the two players and rolled slowly across the goal line.

The devastating goal forced Royals General Manager Sherif Shehata into a ranting frenzy. Owner Mo Sheta was more subdued. His silent nods as he sat on a bench near the field spoke of quiet dismay. Pascarella spent many distraught moments sitting on the bench, his head buried in his hands. Comforting pats on his back by a few players seemed to do little to ease Pascarella's pain.

"Same thing as last week," said defender Adam Vigon to no one in particular. "We just lost six points."

Later, he tried to appease Gonzalo. "I'm sorry, sir," said Vigon. "We deserved (the win). We played wonderful football."

The team showed signs of pure dejection minutes later in the locker room, as if they had just felt their season slip through their weakening grip. Ogando sat in stunned silence on a bench, his soiled uniform a reminder of a hard-fought battle that had ended once again in defeat. Pascarella, who had apologized to Gonzalo as he walked into the locker room, now lay inert on the floor, staring at the ceiling. The locker room reeked of an unsettling quiet, as if the players sensed the team's death. With a playoff position at stake, they had lost three games in a row, losing two after relinquishing late leads. It was clearly their worst defeat of the season.

Gonzalo calmly tried to raise their sunken spirits. "I know the way you're feeling," he said. "I don't know what to tell you. I don't know what happened. We are unlucky. We played to lose in the last few minutes. We have to be a little more, maybe, eager. We need to be more angry. I guess we take things too easy. You were the better team. You played a great game. I am proud of you. Personally, I feel sorry for you. We have three games we have to win. Playing like this, we will."

A GOOD SIGN

During my four days in Phoenix in late July at the U.S. Youth Soccer National Championships, I did not intend to play any soccer. That week, my sore Achilles tendons felt a bit better and before I left for Phoenix I enjoyed good workouts on two of the three days I practiced with the team. The practice on Wednesday was a solid struggle. I spent three long days at work trying to finish some assignments before I departed for Arizona. Through most of the season, work rarely forced me to feel fatigued at practice. But by the time Wednesday's practice arrived, I was wiped out and had little desire to play. It was good, in a sense; it allowed me to experience what the players endured after a tough couple of days at the office.

I figured the chance to get a game in Phoenix would be difficult and planned instead to perform two days of fitness training in a pool. The rest would be good for my aching tendons.

But sometimes the lure of playing just a small-sided game on a plush field is too great. As it turned out, the adidas folks working the tournament, including Royals mate Chris Jones, had called a game for 1 p.m. on Saturday on one of the game fields.

Due to the searing late morning and afternoon heat in Phoenix, games at the youth championships ended by 10 a.m. and started after 5:30 p.m. When the eight of us gathered on Field 3, the temperature rose above 105 degrees. As hot as it was in Phoenix, it felt better than training in the July heat and humidity of Washington, D.C.

It was just the workout I needed: many touches on the ball, a good bit of sprinting and not much stress on the ankles. The brief bits of hard running I did during the one-hour game were only mildly stressful. I played in flats to ease the discomfort. The smooth field's cushiony Bermuda grass enhanced my playing pleasure that day.

I returned to Virginia about 6:30 p.m. on Monday and debated whether or not to attend that evening's Royals practice. I felt a bit weary from the trip but convinced myself to go for one main reason: the following weekend's game against the winless Eastern Shore Sharks was my best chance to play for the Royals. Even if I lagged through practice, at least my attendance would show a commitment to the team.

I arrived at practice at 7:30, in time for a little warm-up and to take part in a shooting drill. I attempted to run a series of 50-meter sprints on my own at the end of practice, but I stopped after a few of them because the tenderness in my Achilles tendons prevented me from getting high on my toes on the rock-hard practice pitch.

I clearly struggled at the practice, but it was crucial that I had attended. After practice, Gonzalo called me over toward the bleachers for a personal chat. When a coach wants to talk to you one-on-one after a practice, it's either that they want to cut you or tell you that you will play a game.

Since it would not behoove the Royals to cut me — can you imagine the kind of book I would write? — I sensed that Gonzalo had some good news for me. He did. He told me to call Shehata to find out about an available roster spot for the Eastern Shore game. But he urged me to call quickly because another Royals player was told of the opportunity as well.

I departed the practice field post-haste to call Shehata on my mobile phone, which I thought was in my car. Typically, when I needed it most, I left it home. The last time I felt so anxious about the Royals was when I drove home from the Media Day back in early April. As then, I felt I could not get home fast enough. I would have been tremendously disappointed if the other player had secured the roster spot.

I called Shehata as soon as I ran into my house. He responded with mild surprise when I talked to him.

"Sheriff, Silvino told me to call you about the roster spot for the game this weekend," I said.

"Really?" he said. There was a moment of silence. "Okay, I'll look into it." I felt a bit uneasy. Did management not want me to play?

He called back a couple of minutes later to verify if Gonzalo wanted me for the Royals game or its reserve team.

I confirmed that it was for the Royals. He then explained that rosters are supposed to be sent in by Monday night for the following weekend's games. We were cutting it close, but he said he thought it would be okay.

After practice the next day, John Ormassa told me that there were in fact two open roster spots for the game and there was a good chance I would be placed on the roster. He suggested I call the league's media relations office to see if they could assure me that they accepted my addition to the roster past the deadline. Ormassa would bring a contract to be signed after practice two days later.

When I called the league office the following day, on Wednesday, I was told that everything was set up. Infused with excitement about finally suiting up, I had my best practice in weeks the next day, although I struggled early. During a 15-minute game of one-and-two touch keep away at the beginning of practice, my touch on the ball felt soft and I hit several weak passes. It was difficult to concentrate.

Still, I felt pumped up when we broke off into a full-field game for 20 minutes. Gonzalo put me up front and I took the opportunity to convince him that I should play against the Sharks. I made repeated runs to the corners and tried to apply annoying pressure to the backs. My Achilles tendons were sore, but the best they had felt in three weeks. All the pool running and weight training maintained good strength in my legs. And my cardiovascular capacity was fine.

We ended practice with a series of five sprints that began at midfield on one touchline, ran along the touchline, around the corners and the goal and ended at the other side of midfield. After each sprint, we (there were two groups) walked across the field to the starting point and began another sprint. I ran the sprints as hard as I could, although I slowed down as I rounded the corners to ease the pain of pivoting while I turned. I finished each sprint among the top three in my group. It hurt good.

As I walked off the field, assistant coach Matt Badiee approached me to comment on my play in the full-field game. "You were all over the field," he said. "That was real good to see. It looked like you were having a lot of fun. That's what this league really is about. Having a lot of fun."

All season, Badiee's mellow personality balanced Gonzalo's fiery approach to the game. He was a good buffer when Gonzalo occasionally erupted to a point of impassioned hysterics.

At the end of a practice in May, a couple of days after the Royals lost three games in three days in New England, Gonzalo decided to put his team through a series of punishing sprints. Not one player, it seemed, fully understood Gonzalo's directions, given in highly accented Spanish, on how to run the sprints. They seemed to comprehend, though, that it was too taxing considering their recent game schedule. Badiee, standing close to the players, settled the matter quickly and calmed down the team when he reduced the number and length of the sprints.

As we walked off the field following the practice before the Sharks game, he made me feel good about all the work I had done all season.

"Silvino made a point to me that you've been one of the players showing up regularly at practice," he said. "You should be proud of that."

Even if I were to never play a game for the Royals, that statement by Badiee justified my season-long efforts and sacrifices. I did not expect to overly impress anyone with my technical skills. But if I had failed to show them a high level of dedication, I would have been greatly disappointed.

Badiee's comment also perplexed me a bit. Was a measure of a player's worth in a professional league determined as much by his level of commitment and loyalty as for his degree of skill? Dennis Rodman does not play a lot for the Chicago Bulls because he has impressed his coaches with an unrivaled level of dedication. They put up with his immaturity because he helps them win games. Perhaps due to the team being unable to pay players, Gonzalo and Badiee tried to instill a more fun attitude within the team. I certainly was not going to argue with that approach.

No other setting promoted team unity and camaraderie for some Royals players better than a coffee house. Almost equally as important as finding a suitable field on which to practice was finding a field located near a Starbucks Coffee shop. Gonzalo and a core of players congregated regularly after practice at the trendy bastion of bold, bean-enhanced brew.

About two months into the season, the site of the Royals practice facility was switched from Potomac, Maryland to McLean, Virginia. I wondered if Gonzalo picked the practice site in Potomac because he knew a nearby shopping center included a Starbucks.

After the first practice in Virginia, goalkeeper John Pascarella, a regular post-practice coffee drinker, immediately addressed a team concern.

"Does anyone know where the nearest Starbucks is?" he asked eagerly. Someone did and within ten minutes about a half dozen of the Royals regulars sat contentedly, their cups of cappuccino and mixes of mocha cradled in their hands, at a Starbucks within one mile of the practice field. It was quite a fortunate coincidence. Or was it?

Initially, I was bewildered that after a physically draining practice a professional athlete would consume beverages that were not only warm but also diuretics. Caffeine actually depletes the body of liquids. I eventually realized that the liquid refreshment was not the main attraction.

Starbucks provided a hip, comfortable environment where tensions and differences between teammates and coaches dissipated as quickly as the steam rising from the brews. Starbucks was the place to boast about your favorite foreign soccer club; to debate the pros and cons of an antiquated league rule; to chat about rifts in personal relationships; to laugh about a comrade's quirks. It promoted team unity. It was appropriate, then, that I signed my first and only professional sports contract in the Starbucks Coffee Shop on Old Chain Bridge Road near downtown McLean, Virginia.

As I signed the document, I wondered how the players felt about me becoming an active player. Did they resent me taking a roster spot that should probably go to another player? Did they fear what would happen if I entered the match?

I tried to hide my discomfort with the situation and also showed little or no emotion. A stoic response might even imply that signing a professional athlete's contract was something I did on a regular basis.

As I signed the document, Adam Vigon walked by and gave me a "thumbs up," easing any silly anxiety I felt.

I felt a mixture of contentment and elation later that evening when I sat down to reflect on the momentous day. I felt content that all my hard work might pay off. In two days I would wear the royal blue and gold of the Northern Virginia Royals. I felt elation that with any luck, the Royals would handily beat the worst team in the league and I would see some substantial playing time.

By the end of the evening, I also felt sadness. I knew playing with the Royals would create some personal conflicts. Earlier in the season, Gonzalo asked me if I wanted to play in an exhibition game against the U-19 Bolivian National Select Team in late June. The game fell on Father's Day weekend. I decided to visit my dad, who is 81, although I realized at the time I may be missing the best chance to play all season.

The Sharks game in August was scheduled for the same weekend an annual Ungrady family gathering was to take place at the New Jersey shore. I would have to miss the big family weekend. The disappointment extended to my 11-year-old nephew Kevin Cahn, who is also my godson. While spending that week at the beach house, he heard I would not be heading north that weekend.

When I got home, I heard the following message from Kevin—a pretty damn good, scrappy midfielder—in my voice mail box: "I hope you're having a good time. All of us really miss you up here and we hoped you could make it. We hope you get to play in your game."

My eyes watered as I listened to the message a couple of times. He cared less about his disappointment than about me achieving a selfish goal. With his blessing, I made a promise to myself not to let him down.

BEWARE OF THE SHARKS

The winless Eastern Shore Sharks must have felt like they were drowning in murky waters. A first-year franchise like the Royals, the Sharks consisted mostly of players from the Baltimore-Washington, D.C. area. As a result, the Sharks practiced just once a week with only about half the players attending since the commute to the Eastern Shore is at least two hours each way. Thirty-one different players started for the team during the season. Like the Royals, none of the players, coaches or management were paid. One of the owners, Kevin Darcy, was also the president, the head coach and a starting defender.

When I told him I was writing a book about the Royals' first year, Darcy laughed good-naturedly.

"You should write a book about us," he said. "We'd give you plenty to write about." It had gotten so bad that if he could not find new owners for 1999, the team would probably fold (they did find new owners and will play in 1999).

Entering the game with the Royals, the Sharks had been outscored for the season, 90-20. They lost games 10-2 and 8-1. The closest they came to a victory was a 2-1 overtime loss to the South Jersey Barons in June. The Sharks had lost 3-2 to the Royals on May 24.

The Sharks faced the Royals for the second time on August 2, closing out their home schedule and hoping for their first win of the season against the team nearest them in the Atlantic division standings. The next weekend, they would close their 1998 campaign against the division-leading Delaware Wizards.

The Royals walked into the locker room at Wicomico County Stadium relaxed despite their tenuous situation—one more loss and they were out of contention for the playoffs. There were a few awkward moments of isolated silence and introspection that typically fill a locker room before a game, but those moments were brief. The players mostly joked and bantered lightly.

Flatulence and its related bodily function—a bowel movement—generated the most laughter. Some fool with poor foresight had designed the relic of a men's locker room—players hung clothes on hooks hanging in rows on the wall; old, rickety, wooden benches on the floor and one-foot wide wooden shelves near the ceiling lined the room—with just one commode.

He must have had little experience as an elite athlete. Men getting primed for athletic battle think of various ways to calm jittery nerves. They take brief naps, read a book, chew tobacco or shake their leg while sitting in place and staring straight ahead, to name a few. Most require at least one visit to the throne of digestive thunder.

Rachid Mahboub was the first to visit the toilet and he immediately transformed the poorly ventilated locker room into a zone of pungent imprisonment. The expected and lighthearted groans and moans followed, as did a continuous procession of hyper-boweled athletes. I typically make two or three trips to the john before a contest, so I needed unimpeded access. Before the locker room opened, I found that the stadium's only men's bathroom was already open and enjoyed movement number one in pensive silence. When movement number two erupted a half hour later, I quietly walked out of the locker room, around the corner and into the bathroom for another grand moment of silence while the commode crush continued in the locker room.

But not everything was flowing smoothly. By 1 p.m. the Royals' rostered goalkeepers had not appeared. John Pascarella did not travel with the team. Rather, he drove to the stadium with his wife. Back-up Dia Kuykendall was still sleeping when the team departed from the rendezvous point in Tysons Corner at 9:30. He said later that his alarm clock failed to go off after power cut off in his residence. It would take him at least two hours to arrive at the stadium.

At 1:10 p.m., Steve Gill tried to make light of the possibility that the team might not have a regular keeper.

"Hey, Dave, what are you like in goal?"

"My hands are okay, but I'm not that mobile."

"We're used to that."

It was an obvious jab at the slow-footed Pascarella.

Almost on cue, Pascarella appeared in the parking lot and rushed to get dressed.

The Royals remained relaxed on the field. During pregame warm-ups, there was barely a trace of the tension that is normal before a game against a more accomplished opponent. After assistant coach Matt Badiee — standing in goal taking shots while Pascarella dressed and Kuykendall was somewhere between the Bay Bridge and Salisbury, Maryland, the location of the Sharks stadium — yelled to Gonzalo to notice a rock-and-roll song blaring on the loudspeaker, Gonzalo bent his knees slightly, criss-crossed his hands and knocked his knees together, mimicking a silly dance routine.

I felt relaxed and confident that if I got in the game I would not embarrass myself. But a couple pregame incidents gave an impression that maybe my nerves were a bit more frazzled than I was willing to admit.

First, I fell over the ball once while trying to make a simple spin move. I'm sure many players have seen this, and some may even have fallen victim to it. You're a bit jazzed with adrenaline flowing and you try something you probably should not try. I tried stepping over the ball with the lead leg, pivoting on that leg and then brushing the bottom of my other foot over the ball to move it towards me as I spun. My first step over the ball was too shallow and, thus, the leather of my boot stuck to the hard finish of the ball.

Fwoomp! I landed hard on my side, but rose promptly to avoid further embarrassment.

Toward the end of pregame, I attempted to punt back onto the field a ball that ended up about 20 yards behind the goal. In my haste, I failed to account for the towering pine tree in my path. The ball soared about 10 yards before becoming implanted about 30 feet up onto a sturdy branch.

The fact that there were only about 10 spectators in the bleachers offered some consolation.

Some intensity prevailed during pregame, however. Moments before the teams took to the field, Engelfried yelled to the group of Royals players assembled for one last cheer.

"Let's bury them early."

Tim Prisco listened well. At the 25-second mark, Prisco almost nonchalantly banged a header in the goal, converting a perfect cross by Alberto Ogando from near the right corner. Gill, from his central defensive position just inside the midfield stripe, had lofted a nice ball to Ogando, who collected the ball on the right flank and ran unobstructed to the corner.

Suddenly, I was thinking that the game was going to be a 6-0 blowout and I might play a good 45 minutes.

But the Royals soon showed how a lack of intensity can result in sloppy play on the field, even against an inferior opponent. Gonzalo's mood became dark by the fifth minute following some inept passing, trapping and a general lack of hustle. The Sharks took advantage of the lapse and scored in the 10th minute following a defensive breakdown in the box.

By the end of the half, the Royals scored twice more and should have scored at least three more. Mark Vita converted after a casual run down the middle of the field and a shot to the upper right corner from just outside the box. Mahboub made a more hasty and challenged run down the left flank, clumsily beat two defenders and toe-poked a shot into the net from about 10 yards out.

The Royals hit a goal post four times, twice by Vita, before the half ended. Another shot, taken superbly by Gill from about 40 yards out with about 15 seconds left in the half, was knocked away by the keeper at the last moment and glanced off the crossbar.

Still, the team was showing little cohesion and hustle on the field defensively. At one point, Gill told Vita to "shut the fuck up and play" following a poor defensive effort on Vita's part.

At half time, Gonzalo emphatically urged his men to keep it simple and told his defense that they were playing too loose.

But the Royals did not expect what would happen soon after the second half commenced. Less than a minute into the half, an unmarked Sharks player collected a through ball behind the Royals defense just outside the box. The Royals waited for the off side call. None came. As Pascarella, standing stunned about 10 yards out of goal, later explained, the player was offside by 10 yards. When he looked to his left for the call from the assistant referee, he saw the referee was sprinting down the touchline to get into position, but was way behind the play.

With no whistle or stoppage of play, the Royals defense was way out of the play and the Sharks player calmly placed the ball behind Pascarella for a goal. For the second straight game, the Royals were burned for a goal on what they claimed was an incompetent no-call on an apparent off side.

The Royals regrouped and had about a dozen more legitimate chances to score before the game ended. Several crafty and long runs by Prisco, ending in 1 v 1 situations with the goalie, proved fruitless.

With 25 minutes left, the Sharks for the first time in the game start-

ed to play with continuous passion and a sense of purpose. They started yelling encouragement to each other. They commanded the midfield and built slow transitions. One could sense that their last regular season home game might be their first win.

The Royals, conversely, marked poorly in central midfield and seemed confused in their defensive third. I stood behind the bench most of the game to calm edgy nerves and try to keep my aching Achilles tendons loose. It was all for naught. With about 15

The author stretches his Achilles tendons as he waits impatiently to make his professional debut.

minutes left and the Royals struggling to put the opponents away, I accepted the fact that I would not play in the game. Initially, I was disappointed and wondered if my only chance to play a professional soccer game had expired due to the futile play of my comrades. Then I thought, hey, if the Sharks score and the game goes into a shoot-out, the season, for all practical purposes, would be over.

My selfish thoughts then quickly transpired to those of support for the team. This was no way to end a season, even one as traumatic as this had been. Let the lads have another chance at completing a dramatic run to the playoffs.

Then, disaster nearly struck — twice. With seven minutes remaining, a Sharks player suddenly found himself unmarked and with the ball merely eight yards in front of the goal. The entire season suddenly flashed before the collective eyes of the bench. But the player launched a missile that soared clearly over the crossbar.

With about one minute remaining and the Sharks pressing, the Royals bench started yelling its displeasure at what it felt were incompetent calls by the referees.

This did not please the Sharks keeper, who was far out from his goal and within close hearing range of the Royals bench.

"Hey, we practice once a week," he said. "And we don't get paid. What are you guys complaining about?"

He won the argument about the one practice a week. But he obviously was misinformed or just naive about the Royals' payment situation. Kuykendall, who arrived at the bench about 10 minutes into the game, would have none of it. He led a flurry of vocal displeasures back to the keeper before a couple of level-headed players convinced him to leave it alone.

And, hey fellas, a game was still going on down at the other end. During the heated verbal transaction, the Sharks won a free kick just outside the box. The attempt failed, but the ball bounced free to just inside the box on the right side. With some 30 seconds remaining in the game, the ensuing shot hit the underside of the crossbar and bounced down but a couple of yards in front of the goal line before Pascarella scooped up the ball. Near disaster was miraculously averted.

With the 3-2 win, the lingering life of the 1998 Northern Virginia Royals was extended at least another five days. The Royals faced the Roanoke Wrath the following Friday. A loss would end the Royals' season. A win would put them two points behind the Wilmington Hammerheads, whom they would face the following Sunday. Should the Royals beat the Wrath, the game against the Hammerheads would decide the sixth and final spot for the playoffs.

Gonzalo showed no compassion following the game. His locker room chat foreshadowed a hellish week.

"I hope you guys think differently this week," he said. "I'll be honest. You have us by the neck. I must pray. We will practice Monday, Tuesday, Wednesday and Thursday. I expect everybody to practice four days this week. And those players on the bench today, if you have long faces, I don't want you. I can't play everybody. If you are unhappy with that, then you must go. I hope you are not happy with this performance."

I tried to stay focused on the prospects of the team and tried to shield my disappointment at not playing. I did not resent Gonzalo for not subbing me in. All he promised me earlier is that he would try to get me in. This game ultimately did not present an opportunity.

Adam Vigon showed true class when he walked up to me as I absorbed the scene sitting on the bench moments after the game; he apologized for the team's poor performance. Vigon had showed the most excitement about my playing pursuits and realized that a rout would have improved my chances of getting in the game.

But all seemed not lost. While placing my bag in the back of the team van as we prepared to depart, Gonzalo apologized for not putting me in the game. But he said he had no choice.

"Maybe against Roanoke," he said. "We will try again next weekend."

THE FINAL WEEKEND, IN PICTURES

PREPARATION – A light workout — a small-sided game for about 45 minutes on a quarter of the field with cones as goals — consumed most of the practice the day before the Roanoke game (right). Towards the end of practice, coach Gonzalo makes notes about the roster for the weekend's games (below). Goalkeeper John Pascarella, who decides not to make the trip because he had an appointment to see if his wife was pregnant, gathers the players after practice and thanks them (middle). He said, "This might be our last practice. I

want to thank you guys for a great year. For guys my age, I don't have many days left like this. Hopefully we will have one more weekend. I know I can be a big pain in the ass. Thanks for putting up with me."

Coach Gonzalo offers final encouraging words to his team at practice the day before the Roanoke game (left). Later, in the parking lot, he said, "The last time we played Roanoke we won because we marked them great and put pressure on the ball. If we do that tomorrow night, we will beat that team 3-0." Leaning on his car, an old Toyota Corolla, he then looked up at the sky, smiled and said, "God, look at me. Is that a hand coming out of the sky or a cloud?"

ON TO ROANOKE—The team had planned to leave Loehmann's Plaza in Falls Church, Virginia by 11:30, but a few players arrived late and delayed the departure (right). While waiting, Adam Wilson declares peace as Elias Christian looks on. While waiting in the parking lot, coach Gonzalo said, "I hate this. I just like to go. We have a game at 7:30, we have to check in yet. This is a big game. I like for them to relax before the game."

The team left the parking lot at 12:10. Some four hours later, the team arrived at its hotel in Roanoke (bottom). From left, Steve Gill, Alberto Ogando, Elias Christian and Chris Jones wait to check in.

THE ROYALS FACE ROANOKE (PRE GAME) – Chris Jones, Alberto Ogando, Dia Kuykendall and Tony Trepal (left to right) relax in the locker room before the game (right). The mood was surprisingly loose considering the game's significance. At one point, coach Gonzalo said jokingly, "Boys, I have good news for you. Mark Vita is going to be my son-in-law." Matt Ferry practices a pregame tradition—shining the boots (far right). Adam Vigon, Tony Trepal and Alberto

Ogando (left to right) pick their kits out of a pile, part of the pre-game routine for the Royals (below, near). Coach Gonzalo and Mark Simpson, on loan from

D.C. United for the weekend, on the field during the pregame warm-up (below, far).

HALF TIME – Tied 0-0 , Gonzalo again expresses his frustration about poor marking at midfield during the half time talk (top). Mark Simpson opines (right). The Royals break from a team huddle moments before the second half began (below). In the 46th minute, former Washington Mustang Greyson Prillaman scored for Roanoke after his shot from the left side of the box deflected off of Alberto Ogando and bounced into the net. The Wrath led, 1-0.

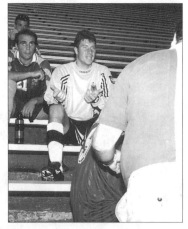

IT'S OVER – Justin Kerns shows his frustration after leaving the game towards the end with his team down 2-0 (top). Roanoke scored its second goal off a penalty kick following a Royals hand ball in the box. As the final minutes evaporated, team owner Mo Sheta, standing behind the bench, calmly lamented about his team's poor performance. "There's no support in mid-

field behind the long balls," he said. "They're not fit, mentally and physically. What this team needs is a true sweeper and regular keeper. (Chris) Jonesy's never here. Rick (Engelfried, playing sweeper against Roanoke), needs to be up front. He's our goal scorer." Their season decided, Steve Gill (standing) and teammates, left to right, Matt Ferry, Rich Engelfried, Alberto Ogando and Leonardo Thiombiano absorb the mood moments after the final whistle (below). Some post-game tension ultimately prevailed. Reserve goalkeeper Dia Kuykendall let erupt his frustration about his infrequent playing time. After Kuykendall told some teammates he thought they played poorly, a couple players tried to calm him down. He then

went face-to-face with Gill, pointing his finger toward Gill's chest and yelling, "Yeah, I'm pissed. I've been showing up everyday and I haven't been playing." Chris Jones, who missed much of the latter part of the season due to work commitments, made light of the moment a little later in the shower. "It's like I've never been gone," he said. After emotions calmed, coach Gonzalo kept his words sparse. "I think you guys were unlucky," he said.

ROANOKE TO WILM-INGTON, N.C. — Somewhere between Raleigh and Wilmington, Rachid Mahboub reads *Soccer America* magazine (top). On travel day the Royals enjoy a relaxed team meal at the Golden Corral just west of Raleigh, N.C. (right). A couple hours later, Mahboub

tries to relax in the van in Wilmington while a few players and I try to find the rest of the team (bottom). As a result of poor communication between management and me, six of us were stranded in Wilmington while—unknown to us—the rest of the team was in Jacksonville, some 45 miles north of Wilmington.

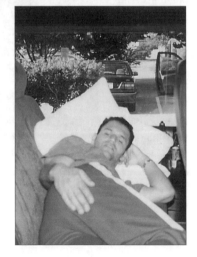

THE ROYALS VERSUS THE HAMMERHEADS (PREGAME)

– Some intensity prevailed in the locker room despite the fact that the Royals' playoff hopes had expired. From left to right: Justin Kerns, Elias Christian, Chris Jones and Adam Wilson (top). With ominous storm clouds hovering, Mo Sheta and coach Gonzalo walk towards the bench minutes before the final game (left). Rain started with the game's first kick. Moments later lightning flashed and thunder roared too close for everyone's comfort. Six seconds into the match, the game was suspended. The referee allowed one hour for the weather to clear before the game would be canceled unless both teams decided otherwise. Players and spectators walk briskly off the field and seek dry comfort (bottom).

RAIN DELAY – Royals players pass the time while the rain falls incessantly for about 45 minutes. Chris Jones shoots hoops while teammates lounge (top). Rachid Mahboub (left), and Kareem Sheta (right) watch as Mahboub's strike finds its target—the backside of a bent-over teammate—during a game of "ass" (middle). In the locker room, Mark Vita (back right, facing) looks at Alberto Ogando as he talks about the adventures of the previous day and night spent away from the team in Wilmington with teammates, from left: Steve Gill, Rick Engelfried, manager Patrick Berkebile, and Adam Wilson (below).

THE END – Moments after the final whistle, Matt Ferry (left) and Alberto Ogando recover from the day's oppressive heat following a 3-1 loss to the Hammerheads. The Royals lost five of their last six games for an overall 7-15 record. They missed the playoffs and finished seventh of eight teams in their division. After the game, players dressed quietly and congenially before they gathered for a final team meal. By 6:30 p.m. they were on the road heading north back to Northern Virginia, their first season already a vivid memory.

WAYWARD IN WILMINGTON

When coach Gonzalo asked me to drive one of the team vans for the last weekend road trip of the season, I had already proven myself worthy of the assignment. About one month earlier, Sheta asked me to drive a van to Roanoke for an away game against the Wrath in mid June. The request made sense; I wanted to write about the game and Sheta kindly offered me a hotel room for the night the team spent in Roanoke after the game.

But after what transpired during the Roanoke-Wilmington trip, I'm sure Sheta won't ask me to chauffeur a team van again. And I would not blame him.

While boarding the vans to leave the hotel the day after the second loss to Roanoke in mid-August, Gonzalo asked me if I knew where we were going. Although I was not certain, I foolishly said yes. I knew we were playing Wilmington, North Carolina, so I figured we would stay there.

I also figured I would ask for further directions when we stopped for gas a few minutes later. But, a whole five minutes went by between leaving the hotel and getting the gas. I forgot to follow up on the directions.

In retrospect, the entire impending mess could have been avoided if each driver (the team traveled in a caravan of five vehicles—two vans and a sports utility vehicle for the players, a station wagon with an assistant and a player and Sheta driving in a car with his son) was given written directions. That was the case during the previous trip to Roanoke and the traveling went flawlessly. As it turned out, some vehicles did have directions to the team hotel in North Carolina; I did not.

A few minutes after leaving the gas station, I spotted Sheta to my left as we sped along highway 220 South just a couple of miles from the hotel in Roanoke. While cruising along at about 60 miles per hour, I rolled down my driver-side window and waited for Sheta's son, Kareem, sitting in the passenger seat, to roll down his window.

"Where are we staying?" I yelled through the rustling wind.

Sheta directed his son to ruffle through some papers. After about 20 seconds of confusion, Kareem yelled back to me.

"The Comfort Suites."

"What street?"

"Piney Green."

I did not ask in what city the hotel was located. I assumed it was Wilmington. After all, we were going to play the Wilmington Hammerheads.

Ooops #1.

There is no Comfort Suites and no Piney Green road or street in Wilmington. That's because the hotel is in Jacksonville, some 45 miles north of Wilmington.

I must clarify that I place no blame on Kareem Sheta. A boy of nine cannot be held responsible while acting as a conduit for information between two adults. The blame for not getting better directions falls squarely on me.

By the time the team vehicles had reached the exit for Jacksonville, our van—which included Mark Vita, Dia Kuykendall, Maxx-Henry Frazier, Rachid Mahboub, Adam Wilson and me—was the only one separated from the Royals caravan. My driver's license was on probation for excessive moving violations and I did not want to risk another ticket by keeping up with the other Royals drivers at 85 miles per hour.

Our wayward van wandered into Wilmington at about 5 p.m. By 5:30, we found no Comfort Suites, but not for a lack of trying. A call to telephone information yielded no Comfort Suites in Wilmington.

Wilson called home and obtained Sheta's beeper number, which he immediately called. While waiting for a return call from Sheta on my mobile phone, we cruised through most of commercial Wilmington looking for team vans in hotel parking lots and for a Comfort Suites. No luck, although some excitement flowed through the van when we spotted a Hooters Restaurant.

Ah, success? We spot a Comfort Inn. Certainly, they must know something. No Comfort Suites in Wilmington. We never thought of asking if there is a Comfort Suites in Jacksonville because we didn't think we were supposed to be in Jacksonville.

We then made more calls—a couple more beeps to Sheta, to Royals team owners and management in Northern Virginia, to Wilmington team owners and management, to dozens of hotels in Wilmington. Of the one dozen or so calls—except to the hotels in Wilmington—only one yielded a live human voice. Tim Schweitzer, a Royals marketing assistant, said he would talk to his wife upon her return to find out where the team was staying. We never heard back from them.

Goalkeeper Dia Kuykendall made his second appearance of the season in the Royals last game.

It was now about 6:30. We needed food and to find a hotel in case we would be stuck in Wilmington. The league media guide lists the hotel for each team, so I thought maybe that hotel would help us locate the team. But I did not have the media guide. I called Brian Straus, a company editorial assistant, in Alexandria, Virginia. He quickly located the media guide and the name of the hotel—the Fairfield Inn.

Each team is required by the league to make arrangements with a hotel to provide seven rooms for the visiting team. The folks at the Fairfield Inn were a bit confused that the Royals were not staying at their hotel, since they had accommodated other visiting teams that season. That should have told us something.

Still, the fine people at Fairfield could not have been more helpful. They agreed to hold two rooms for us until 10 p.m. By that time, I was hoping we would hear from the team.

With rooms secured, the six of us went across the street to Bennigan's Restaurant for dinner. During the season, the players were careful about not drinking alcohol the night before a game. Gonzalo adamantly made the team aware that drinking the night before a game was disallowed. But since the season, for all intents and purposes, was over, there was no trepidation by some of the players to toss down a few alcoholic beverages of choice.

While we dined at the bar, Vita's humor and Kuykendall's worldly rap soon caught the attention of two female bartenders. The bartenders even seemed impressed that they were serving professional soccer players, a fact brought into the conversation by the players rather quickly.

Since I was almost twice the age of the players, I tried to play the role of chaperone. During the next two hours, I made nearly a dozen more calls and beeps to Royals and Hammerheads management. No calls were returned while at the bar.

We checked into the hotel by 10 p.m. Wilson, Henry-Frazier and I decided to stay in for the night. Wilson spent most of the night talking to his girlfriend on the phone, Henry-Frazier is too young too drink and I wanted to get as much rest as possible for my likely professional debut.

Vita, Kuykendall and Mahboub had other ideas. The lovely bartenders persuaded them to venture to a bar near the beach, about 10 minutes away. The game the next day was the farthest thing from their minds.

We finally received a phone call in our room from Gonzalo at about midnight. When I took the receiver, I felt embarrassed and a bit humbled by our misadventure. But I also felt a bit betrayed by team management. Why hadn't they returned our calls? Did they really care?

Apparently they did. Gonzalo first wanted to know how we got lost and then adequately expressed the team's concern for us.

"We called the police," he said. "We thought something happened to you guys."

I tried to defend our continuous efforts to contact the team, telling him we had tried repeatedly to beep Sheta and contact other team management.

Then Gonzalo wanted to survey the status of his players.

"Did any players go out?"

I hesitated before answering. I quickly rationalized that Gonzalo is no dummy. Would some of these six highly-sociable athletes, on a road trip and dislocated from the team and their coach, engage in a bit of unrestricted social activity? Of course.

If I lied and said no, Gonzalo probably would ask to talk to the other guys. So I tried the honest approach.

"Yes."

"Who?"

"Mark, Dia and Rachid."

"Tell them they're benched tomorrow."

Ooops #2.

We then agreed to talk more the next morning at the team's hotel in Jacksonville before the game.

Motivated by guilt (I'm Catholic; we feel guilty about everything) for having finked on my teammates, I quickly jumped into the team van to find the players and warn them of their dilemma. Within 15 minutes I found them sardined amid a festive crowd in an oceanside bar, enjoying their freedom and their newfound friends.

Once I saw their faces—most notably Vita's incessant, illuminated and devilish grin, looking like a jolly George Clooney—I sensed that it would take much more than a coach's threat to pry them away from their fun.

I had to yell to combat the incessant and booming percussive music. "Mark, I just want to warn you," I said. "I don't know what you want to do, but I just talked to Silvino and he said you guys are benched tomorrow. He asked me if any players went out and I told him you guys did."

For a moment, Vita looked stunned. Mahboub was several feet behind Vita and unable to hear me and thought I was there to join the party. He offered me a beer, but I declined. Kuykendall was in between the two, trying to gauge my appearance.

"Dave," Vita said, a look of pure mischievousness on his face. "You never saw us."

At about nine the next morning, Henry-Frazier and I were feasting on the hotel's complimentary and tremendously adequate breakfast (my meal consisted of French toast, yogurt, orange juice and a banana) in the hotel lobby when in walked Vita looking as if he had body-surfed all night. His cropped hair was a bit matted and his eyes were barely open. Still, he flashed the trademark grin that seemed to imply a tone of complete indifference to anything normal.

Vita spotted Henry-Frazier and me as he walked toward the food.

"I'm benched today, right?"

"It looks that way," I said.

"Good," he said with fatigued relief.

Henry-Frazier and I got a good chuckle out of that one.

Vita's disinterest in playing was understandable. After the bar closed, Kuykendall and Vita enjoyed a brief session of skinny-dipping in the ocean with one of the bartenders. The swim was cut short after the bathers spotted two headlights from a beach patrol vehicle in the distance. Vita quickly ran from the water, picked up his shorts and sprinted to refuge at a nearby house party. Kuykendall and the bartender hid in a bush until the patrol car passed them.

Vita netted only two hours of sleep; Mahboub and Kuykendall a couple more. And Gonzalo kept his word, sort of.

By the time the Royals headed to Jacksonville, North Carolina to close out their season, their opponent, the Wilmington Hammerheads, had barely secured a spot in the playoffs. The Hammerheads were in sixth place with a 7-10 record, five points ahead of the seventh-place Royals.

While the Hammerheads struggled a bit on the field, they had reached a respectable level of stability as a D3 team. They lost money each of their first three years, including the 1998 season. Hammerheads Director of Operations Shawn Kowalewski hopes to break even in 1999. But making money is not a priority for Wilmington. "Whatever we make goes right back into the youth of the community," said Kowalewski.

The Hammerheads owner, WSAI, Inc., is set up as a non-profit corporation. In addition to the Hammerheads, it operates nine boys and girls youth teams from ages U10 to U-18. Some Hammerheads players coach the youth teams.

Kowalewski estimated that in 1998 the team recovered about three quarters of its expenses, which, he said, were around $300,000; the amount most D3 teams spend per year. During the 1998 season, the Hammerheads averaged about 800 spectators per game compared to 1,400 per game in 1996. Kowalewski blamed poor weather for the decreased attendance.

About 600 spectators, mostly youngsters shrieking constantly to the point of annoyance, filled Jacksonville High School stadium in August for the game against the Hammerheads. I noticed the loud youngsters because I spent most of the game standing behind the bench, waiting nervously to be called into the game.

I felt my chances of playing were solidified after I noticed the three night prowlers sitting the bench at the beginning of the game. I figured that of the three only Kuykendall would play, because he had played very little all season. In that scenario, the maximum four field player substitutions would be available. With five bench players left—Wilson, Vita, Henry-Frazier, Mahboub and me—my chances of playing looked good.

Rachid Mahboub, left, and Mark Vita sat the bench when the game started against the Hammerheads, but they eventually entered the match.

Still, I felt an uneasiness between Gonzalo and me throughout the morning of the game. Gonzalo and I had developed a comfortable friendship. I became fond of his sense of humor and affable personality. After the Royals lost to Richmond, Gonzalo, assistant coach Matt Badiee and I spent part of the evening drinking a few beers at a bar near the hotel. We talked mostly about soccer and women for two hours and most of the conversation was laced with good-hearted laughter.

I shared a room that evening with Gonzalo, Badiee and assistant coach Patrick Berkebile. The four of us acted like a bunch of kids on a sleepover and continued our juvenile banter until around 3 a.m. Gonzalo received ample ribbing for wearing a tidy satin or silk pajama ensemble.

The comfort level between Gonzalo and me seemed altered following the misadventures of the previous evening. Prior to the previous game against Eastern Shore, Gonzalo reminded me repeatedly to bring along my driver's license, which I needed as identification in case I checked into the game.

But as we walked into the locker room before the Hammerheads game one week later, Gonzalo seemed indifferent about my presence. When I gave him my license without him requesting it, he seemed to take it reluctantly. I felt my chances of playing were affected by the mix-up in Wilmington. Gonzalo's threat to bench the curfew violators lasted one half. Kuykendall started the second half, Vita entered the game early in the second half and Wilson entered the game about midway through the second half. Kuykendall played with enthusiasm, yelling directions to his defense and trying to exhort his teammates. But he admittedly misplayed a shot that led to a Hammerheads goal.

The Royals had two substitutions to use with about 20 minutes remaining in the game, and down 3-0. Gonzalo next summoned Henry-Frazier into the match; so the final substitution was going to be either Mahboub or me. Gonzalo had asked Mahboub to warm up with about 30 minutes remaining, but 15 minutes later he was still not in the game. Mahboub then sat on the bench, thinking Gonzalo had changed his mind. Mahboub said later that after he sat down he had no desire to play.

I still thought Gonzalo would finally call me into the game. I looked at the clock every 30 seconds or so, as if my stares of concern could will it to move slower. But with just more than 13 minutes remaining, Gonzalo called Mahboub's name again. As he casually rose off the bench and checked into the match, I tried to hide my disappointment. And I quickly tried to figure out why, with the Royals down 3-1 and very little chance of tying or winning the match, Gonzalo had not called me into the game.

I waited a few days to ask Gonzalo why I did not play. About a week after the last game, I reached him on the phone.

"Silvino, I've got to ask you why I did not play."

"David, I am sorry, I have no explanation."

The response surprised me. I was quiet for a moment.

"Did it have anything to do with us getting lost the night before?"

"No, no. That had nothing to do with it."

I wanted to believe him.

PUT ME IN, COACH

or the record, I made my professional soccer debut with the Royals on September 19, 1998 on an unseasonably warm afternoon. It wasn't a true professional game. The Royals played an All-Star team from the Arlington Soccer League, a predominantly Hispanic amateur league in the Washington, D.C. area.

However, many of the Arlington Soccer League "amateur" players get paid some kind of cash, although usually less than $100 a game. Which, ironically, was about $100 a game more than the Royals "professional" team players earned. So in a sense, it was a professional game.

And although it was an exhibition game that was not sanctioned by the USISL, all the Royals players—including me—had signed professional contracts. I was playing on a team with professionals.

The reason I've taken the time to convince you that it was a professional game is that I need to convince myself it was a professional game. Once I'm convinced it was a professional game, maybe I can finally and officially claim that I was a professional athlete, even if just for a small part of one day. I can then move on to a less physically stressful and time-consuming mode of playing soccer. Like playing in an over-40 league or just kicking a ball against a wall.

After I did not play for the Royals during the season, coach Silvino Gonzalo seemed guilt-ridden. He had tried graciously to find a game for me to play with his team. Gonzalo had asked me to play in an earlier exhibition game after the season, but another family commitment took me out of town.

Gonzalo explained why the Royals set up the game against the Arlington League All-Stars. "We want to do some P.R. within the Hispanic soccer community and we want to have fun," he said. "We want to put on a show." I wondered what kind of show the Royals could put on considering most players had not stayed match fit since the season ended more than a month earlier.

A free kick nearly hits the author, in the middle of the wall, in the face.

It was good to see some of the lads again, even some faces that belonged to bodies that finally healed up and were ready to play. Devin Payton and Jeff Todd, both of whom missed most of the season due to injury, proclaimed a high level of overall fitness but expected to show some match-rust on the pitch.

After the season ended, Gonzalo staged light, once a week, optional practice sessions in the early evening for anyone who wanted to stay somewhat soccer fit. The zesty and loose sessions were simply small-sided games or one- two- and three-touch games of keep-away. The practices attracted from 10 to 20 players.

Aided by increased sessions of physical therapy, my Achilles tendons still ached but were getting stronger. I was able to maintain training on a less strenuous level. I ran once a week, attended all but one of the practices, ran and performed kicking exercises in a swimming pool once a week, worked out on a recumbent bicycle once or twice a week and continued a weight lifting routine. I was determined to maintain the best level of fitness for my eventual debut.

A few of the team regulars—Rick Engelfried, Steve Gill, Mark Vita and Tim Prisco, most of whom did not attend the optional practices—showed up for the game. Gonzalo also invited many new players for a tryout.

The field was surprisingly comfortable considering how hard most of the fields had become due to a severe lack of rain. Dirt was placed over the many bare spots to soften the overused pitch, which possessed its share of bumps and uneven groves. It was a fairly typical public-access field in the Washington, D.C. area.

The soft field eased the discomfort of my still-sore tendons. During warm-ups, I felt a strong pinch to the back of the heel every time either foot hit the ground.

By game time, however, adrenaline and increased blood flow to the sore areas deadened most of the discomfort.

Gonzalo told me at the beginning of half time that I should get ready to play. Did that mean I would start the second half? Would I sub in after the half began? I didn't ask and I didn't care. I was just happy to prepare to play.

During half time, I ran a series of sprints, stretched and worked some quick touches with a teammate. I felt silly getting so excited. The game was meaningless. About 50 people were watching. A few friends attended along with a mostly Hispanic audience. The level of play lacked a prevailing intensity and bore just a sliver of purpose.

By the time I checked in at the start of the second half, the pain in my Achilles tendons became just a mild nuisance. I don't remember what kind of instruction Gonzalo imparted to me. I did know that I would hustle my balls off and cover the right flank with whatever pace I had left in my 40-year-old legs. I was confident I could play a hard 45 minutes.

But the first five minutes felt like an entire game. Due to nervousness more severe than I was aware of, my breathing felt labored and my awareness far from acute. I felt awkward. This reaction—known as the flight or fight response—often results when a well conditioned athlete is placed into an uncomfortable situation. A strong infusion of adrenaline combined with nervousness forces heavier breathing than usual. Blood is therefore pumped harder to the muscles, forcing a loss of sensitivity and control of the nerves.

Elite athletes learn how to handle these situations by taking a couple slow, deep breaths and forcing themselves to focus. This response typically subsides after the athlete becomes more comfortable with the situation.

After a few minutes, I settled down and fell into the flow of the game. I focused on marking the other team's outside midfielder and making runs up the flank to support offensive attacks. The running felt easy and it felt good to mix it up.

A couple of minutes into the half, a high punt by our keeper floated toward the midfield stripe on my side of the field. I ran back to cover it, tilting my head back as I ran to follow the flight of the ball. Battling with an opposing player, I missed my first attempt at the header out of the air, but recovered in time to head it toward a teammate after one bounce.

A few minutes later, I stood in the way of another Arlington player trying to go to goal right near our end line about 20 yards out. I was determined to keep him out of the box. Another Arlington player ran by him. The attacking player, moving forward slowly, suddenly lost possession and the three of us battled for the ball. I dove in feet first, clearing the ball away and falling backward. I had won my first two battles.

But I failed later when finesse was required. Just short of midfield, I feebly hit my first pass, a soft back touch to a supporting player about 10 yards behind me. It was a classic hospital ball, one that makes the player receiving the pass susceptible to an aggressive tackle by a defender. That placed my teammate in a potentially injurious situation. My teammate did not get hurt as the ball reached him at the same time as a defender, but we lost possession of the ball.

A couple of minutes later, I received the ball on the flank in our offensive third. I had a little time to survey the movement up front and saw one of our forwards making a run to the near post. I sent the ball in too hard; it floated behind the defense and landed unthreateningly in the keeper's hands.

I spent most of the time running up and down the flank, covering space and playing defense. After the All-Stars won a free kick just outside the box, I ended up one of four players in the wall. As I turned my head to avoid contact with the ball, the shot zoomed by inches away from my face and sailed over the crossbar.

My most dramatic effort, though, almost resulted in my scoring a goal. After we were awarded a corner kick from the opposite side of the field, I felt myself typically pinching in to my near post. But something told me to back off a bit. The outside midfielder should stand near or outside the 18-

yard line in case a ball floats over everybody's heads.

A defender marked me loosely, about seven yards away. I saw the full flight of the ball from when it was hit. It started low but rose gradually and gained pace as it entered the box. As I moved forward to meet the ball, I sensed that I was in perfect position to bang it in if I managed to correctly time my jump. Since I hadn't practiced such heading in more than a month, that seemed unlikely.

To my benefit, a defender did not contend with me for the ball. All I had to do was run forward to meet it with effective contact without jumping. From about 16 yards out, I headed the ball squarely, but it lacked sufficient pace and proper direction. The ball floated, not soared, just wide right of the near post. It would have been an historic way to end my professional debut with a netter. Gonzalo subbed me out about a minute later.

As I walked away from the play, Mark Vita saw a chance to tease me. "Hey, Dave, next time keep your mouth closed," he said, smiling. "I should open my eyes, too," I replied.

The author running the right flank in his Royals debut.

As I write this—on a mid-November day with temperatures in the mid 60s—the radiantly colorful leaves on the trees have lingered on the limbs longer than usual. Why are they being so stubborn? Why don't they just accept the fact that they should have withered weeks ago? Don't they realize that they'll be back next spring, stronger than ever?

I think I've been spending too much time in front of my computer writing this book and looking at trees.

As the leaves slowly accept the fact that their time has come, so have I regarding my competitive soccer days. I have been walking with a limp for four months. After the Royals season ended, I wanted to take advantage of the fitness I had accumulated into a prolific fall amateur season with the Blackwatch of the Northern Virginia Soccer League's first division. I was willing to endure the nagging discomfort in my Achilles tendons just a couple more months, or at least until I played one game with the Royals.

I stopped playing soccer two weeks ago. My rehabilitation therapist told me that if I tried to play the next day in an amateur game that there was a good chance I would tear the tendons off the bone. The warning sign was a deep ping of pain that shot through the back of my heel bone as his assistant rolled an ultrasound wand around the base of the Achilles tendon.

In a sense, I was relieved. I was unwilling to make the decision myself. Now the decision had been made for me. I vow not to play soccer again until I can run with no discomfort.

Kicking a ball has been replaced with one hour of physical therapy up to five days a week. It includes electric stimulation and ultrasound to reduce swelling and help break up scar tissue, manual massage to increase circulation and flush poisons away and strengthening and flexibility exercises. Running has been replaced with aquatic exercises, in-line skating, Cycle Reebok and no-impact workouts on cardiovascular machines. I look forward eagerly to the day I can run comfortably again.

It was time to accept the fact that I have finally fallen off my soccer tree. But I've managed to grab the last, low-lying limb, where I hang precariously in a state of uncertainty about my soccer-playing future.

One thought is clear, though. By next spring, I hope to blossom stronger than ever.

EPILOGUE

Royals head coach Silvino Gonzalo was asked in late October if he wanted his players back for the 1999 season.

"Right now, I want everyone back," he said.

But Gonzalo may have to look hard for new talent for the Royals' second season. When asked if they would return, most who played frequently said maybe or no, citing dreams of advancement in pro soccer or frustration with no certainty of payment. Five starters—team captain Rick Engelfried, midfielder Alberto Ogando and defenders Justin Kerns, Chris Jones and Steve Gill—said they will definitely return.

Engelfried is not concerned about making money playing with the Royals. "Payment doesn't matter. I definitely will be playing, unless they cut me," he said laughing. "I enjoyed getting back into highly competitive soccer and practicing on a daily basis. But the most difficult thing was not having a lot of preparation time to choose players, and picking a team. We had players come in and out at practice—you really couldn't establish any kind of rhythm. In practice you'd play with guys you'd never play with in a game. And sometimes trips could have been more organized. But I think management did the best they could with the amount of people they had working for them."

Ogando enjoyed his season with the Royals. "It was a little disappointing not making the playoffs, but I had a great time," he said. "I knew what I was getting into before the season started. I wasn't concerned about not making money. I was trying to help get the team off the ground."

Defender Chris Jones would like to play next year, but his availability should again be limited due to job commitments.

Gill said if he does not play for the Royals, he would like to help coach the team.

Kerns is indifferent about the lack of financial compensation. "I'm not worried about the (lack of) money," he said. "I've got a good job that pays the bills. This is kind of a dream for me."

For forward Tony Trepal, the season turned out to be a nightmare. During the season he had captured the admiration of Gonzalo for his toughness. Trepal missed most of the season due to a hamstring injury.

When he did play, he showed gutsy perseverance through pain and was a welcome spark on the forward line.

Trepal said he agreed to a one-year term with the Royals. But when he tried to retain his amateur status in October to play in the National Amateur Cup for an amateur club, L.C.C., he found out that the Royals contract was for three years.

"When I negotiated with the Royals, they wanted me to sign for three years," Trepal said in November. "But I wanted only one year. I was told I would get a copy of the contract, but I never received it."

When his coach at L.C.C. called the U.S. Soccer Federation to check on Trepal's status, he was told that Trepal had signed a three-year deal with the Royals, and was therefore ineligible to play in the Amateur Cup.

"I decided not to mess with it because by the time I would send in the resubmission forms for amateur status, the Cup qualifying would be finished," he said. "I wasn't happy. I haven't been able to play for three weeks because league games stop while Cup games take place."

Trepal doubts he will play for the Royals in 1999. "I'm definitely not planning on coming back," he said. "They'd really have to change the way they do things."

Forward Leonardo Thiombiano said he might return if tryouts with A-League teams—the Maryland Mania, for example—are unsuccessful.

Midfielder Jeff Standish was researching Ph.D. programs after the season. He said his return depends on whether he will be in the Washington area next season and which players return. "I would consider it, although I didn't have a great experience," he said in mid-November. "But I haven't heard from management since the end of the season."

Midfielders Mark Vita, Tim Prisco, Adam Wilson, Rachid Mahboub and Matt Ferry—all in their early or mid-20s—aspire to higher levels of professional play. But they have varied ambitions with the Royals if A-League or MLS opportunities do not materialize.

"If I don't go to a higher league, I will play on a when-I-can capacity," said Vita, who hopes to play in Major League Soccer within two years. "This year I missed a lot of things because of practice. If they pay me, and, depending on what job I have and how much money I need, I might increase my commitment. I love playing: I'll do as much as I can. I think my chances are good to play with an A-League team. I know some people."

Prisco was looking to try out for Major League Soccer. "If that does not work out, I'd like to play for the Royals next year," he said.

Wilson, the recipient of repeated wrath from Gonzalo throughout most of the season, is certain he will be elsewhere in 1999. "There's no way I'll play for the Royals," he said. "I asked Mo (Sheta) for a release (in September) and he said yes." Wilson planned to hire an agent to arrange tryouts with MLS or A-League teams. He said he hoped to get a tryout with D.C. United during the winter.

Mahboub would like to play for an A-League team, but if that does not happen, he would be happy to return to the Royals. "I like the management," he said. "They're good guys."

Ferry earned a master's degree in science and research management in December and plans to be anywhere but in the Washington, D.C. area next spring. "I'm definitely not playing with them," he said. "There was nothing professional about this team. Sometimes we practiced on a baseball field at some rec center. It would have been nice to get practice gear. The little things make a difference, make the team feel and look like a team."

Practice field conditions were a struggle all season for the Royals. They trained on bumpy fields at a recreational complex in Avenel, Maryland, for the first two months before moving to Lewinsville Park in McLean, Virginia. Lewinsville's fields were better maintained, but the Royals were second-class citizens there. They had access to the better fields only when youth teams did not practice. About a half dozen times, the Royals were forced to practice on a front field not set up for soccer. The field was slightly elevated on one side. Bushy trees bordered the lower side. Many balls were lost in that heavy brush and practice was interrupted often to chase balls into the thicket.

Ferry was asked to try out for the Maryland Mania, a new A-League team that begins play in Baltimore in 1999. But he was reluctant to play for another start-up franchise. "Playing for the Royals sucked so much life out of me," he said.

Ferry planned to move to California in January and try out for some A-League teams. "If it doesn't work there, I'm going to jump in my car and find another team to try out for," he said.

There's a chance the Royals will have to look for a new goalkeeper. John Pascarella, who worked as an assistant coach for the University of Maryland in 1998, said he would like to play for the Royals but his availability might be limited. His wife is expecting their first child by early May. Andrew Scogna has recovered from his knee injury and was hoping to get a tryout at the MLS combine. Dia Kuykendall, who played in only two games, moved to California.

Defender Adam Vigon enjoyed playing with the Royals and might return in 1999. "I'm pretty sure I'll be back," said Vigon, an assistant coach at the University of Charleston in West Virginia during the fall. "I had a good time. But it wouldn't be fair to ask everybody to play for nothing again. The guys need to know the club's moving forward."

To be fair, team management faced a tough task in their first season. If they spent too much money, they could have jeopardized the long-term stability of the team. USISL Commissioner Francisco Marcos said it usually takes three years for a D3 team to establish some firm ground. Remember what happened to the Washington Mustangs? They paid players salaries each year and folded after three seasons. Marcos said after the season that the Royals were in good financial standing with the league.

As tough as it was on the players and coaches and to maintain team morale at times, perhaps Royals owner Mo Sheta in the long run will be lauded for being so frugal during the first season.

Sheta spent the fall implementing changes prompted from the learning experiences of the first season. He hopes there will be a big adjustment to their schedule.

"Sunday afternoon games were killers," he said. "We found out that youth players and parents don't want to watch too much soccer on a Sunday afternoon after they've been at youth games all weekend. We learned not to schedule games on the weekend of a tournament unless it's a Friday before the tournament. We don't want to play any home games in April or early May. We can get more youth players at games when their season is over. And we can bring in some international players when their season is over."

The Royals have switched equipment sponsors from Puma to adidas. Sheta hopes that will improve chances of an increased relationship with D.C. United, which is also sponsored by adidas. Sheta also hopes to arrange for one or two Royals games at RFK stadium before D.C. United matches.

D.C. United General Manager Kevin Payne is open to discussion with the Royals. "The first step needs to be them coming to us with ideas," he said.

There's not much the Royals can do about a game field. They might be forced to return to their home pitch at Fairfax High School. The field drains poorly despite low areas and exposed drains on each side of the pitch. Youth soccer leagues and the high school's soccer, football and lacrosse teams all use the field, leaving little time to repair the sod.

"You can't play good soccer there," said D.C. United goalkeeper Mark Simpson, who played several matches with the Royals. "The skill level goes way down playing on that field."

Sheta does not see the game-field situation improving any time soon. "The high schools are reluctant to let us use their fields," said Sheta, who paid around $1,000 per game for the field. "They are overused. The field last year was a struggle and it is going to be a struggle this year. We would like to get involved with D.C. United and build a stadium. We'll just try to make the best of it."

Sheta in October 1998 hired former Richmond Kickers owner Bobby Lennon as the Royals' director of marketing and corporate sales. As of November, Lennon was the only paid employee of the Royals.

"We want to target the corporate community and the youth soccer community," he said in early November. "From January through February, I plan to attend every board meeting at every youth club and tell them about the team. I want the games to be a sideshow to D.C. United. People go to D.C. United games for a different reason. We hope our games will be like a county fair. Mom, dad and the kids can drive 10 to 15 minutes and enjoy a side show along with the game. Maybe we'll have a few carnival-type rides."

Lennon hopes to introduce a promotional tool he used with the

Kickers that integrates Royals practices with youth practices. The Royals would train at different youth team complexes and before or after practice would conduct clinics for the youth players.

"It's a very sensitive issue because you don't want to turn practices into a circus, but these promotions are very important to the Royals," he said. "This worked very well with the (Richmond) Kickers."

As for games, Lennon would like to offer many free tickets to youth players. "We're going to give the first home game away to every youth soccer player in the community if the clubs agree to distribute the information to their members. My aim is to pack the stadium the first night and then offer discounted tickets to two or three youth clubs each game."

Sheta welcomes implementing the new marketing strategy. He says much of what they will try to do in 1999 was already known, but the Royals did not have the resources or time to implement the ideas.

On the field, Sheta will be more involved with the team. "I will be going to practice more and helping the players on the field," he said. "But I don't want to use the words 'assistant coach.'"

The main issue of contention between players and management— paying the players—still lingers. By November, Sheta was not sure if players would receive payment. Sheta said the team lost about $20,000 in operating expenses in 1998.

"It all depends on what we bring in," he said. "I'm not going to pay them out of my pocket. I feel I've already helped them enough."

In early December, the Royals held an open tryout at a community center in Arlington, Virginia. It was one of several held in the fall. More than 30 aspirants showed up, to the delight of head coach Silvino Gonzalo, who invited eight players back for another tryout.

"It was fantastic," he said. "I was very impressed. The skill level was better than our current players. I'm looking for good goalkeepers and two fast central defenders. I think we will have a very good midfield. We will be very good next year. I can't wait."

ROYALS 1998 ROSTER

Players who appeared in at least one league game for the Royals

G	Dia Kuykendall
G	Jan Da Weer
G	John Pascarella
G	Andrew Scogna
G	Mark Simpson
G	Tom Presthus
D	Jeff Todd
D	Brad Agoos
D	Justin Kerns
D	Chris Jones
D	Martin Brillantine
D	Steve Gill
D	Steven Franzke
D	Adam Vigon
D/F	Rick Engelfried
M	Sean Lapier
M	Garth Campbell
M	Matt Ferry
M	Alberto Ogando
M	Mark Vita
M	Elias Christian
M	Devin Payton
M	Tim Prisco
M	El Said Moataz
M	Adam Wilson
M	Jeff Standish
F	Tony Trepal
F	Leo Thiombiano
F	Charlie Raphael
F	Rachid Mahboub
F	Scott Poirier
F	Maxx Henry-Frazier

ROYALS 1998 RESULTS

April 10
ROYALS 3, CEN. JERSEY RIPTIDE 2 (OT)

April 19
W. MASS. PIONEERS 4, ROYALS 0

April 26
DELAWARE WIZARDS 1, ROYALS 0

May 1
READING RAGE 4, ROYALS 1

May 3
ROYALS 1, R. ISLAND STINGRAYS 0 (OT)*

May 16
R. ISLAND STINGRAYS 3, ROYALS 2 *

May 17
CAPE COD CRUSADERS 5, ROYALS 0 *

May 18
N. HAMPSHIRE PHANTOMS 2, ROYALS 1 *

May 24
ROYALS 3, EASTERN SHORE SHARKS 2

May 29
ROYALS 3, S.C. SHAMROCKS 2 (OT)

May 30
CHARLOTTE EAGLES 2, ROYALS 0

June 6
DELAWARE WIZARDS 4, ROYALS 1

June 13
ROANOKE WRATH 2, ROYALS 0

June 21
BOLIVIAN NATIONAL U-19 3, ROYALS 1
(exhibition)

June 26
S.C. SHAMROCKS 2, ROYALS 1

July 8
ROYALS 4, WIL. (N.C.) HAMMERHEADS 2

July 11
ROYALS 2, ROANOKE WRATH 1 (SO)

July 17
MYRTLE BEACH SEADAWGS 3, ROYALS 1

July 18
MYRTLE BEACH SEADAWGS 4, ROYALS 3

July 25
CHARLOTTE EAGLES 4, ROYALS 3 (OT)

August 2
ROYALS 3, EASTERN SHORE SHARKS 2

August 7
ROANOKE WRATH 2, ROYALS 0

August 9
WIL. (N.C.) HAMMERHEADS 3, ROYALS 1

* US OPEN CUP GAMES
FINAL RECORD: 7 wins, 15 losses